My Transition Portfolio

Keys to Unlocking Self-Determination for Young Adults with Disabilities

BARB BLAKESLEE M.ED., NBCT

BOOK PUBLISHERS NETWORK
Changing the World One Book at a Time

My Transition Portolio- Keys to Unlocking Self Determination for Young Adults with Disabilities [SAMPLE COPY]

April 20, 2016

To Whom It May Concern:

As a special education teacher, I knew my students lacked quality resources to prepare them for life after high school. My passion in this field led me to fill this gap, and I developed the enclosed book, *My Transition Portfolio*, for young adults with disabilities, as well as for their caregivers, teachers, and service agency personnel.

My Transition Portfolio assists students in preparing for their future by developing a portfolio, which they share with others, as they transition from their school-based program and enter into adulthood and the world of work. My students use the forms and exercises in the book, and I see how much they benefit.

In addition, through interactions with my students, I see firsthand where to refine the book. Thus I am revising the first edition of *My Transition Portfolio* and am seeking comments about it from those who are influential in transition services for young adults with disabilities. Please accept the enclosed uncorrected copy of *My Transition Portfolio* for your review. I welcome your feedback and perspective on ways to improve the book for these students at this turning point in their lives.

The all-new and fully revised second edition of *My Transition Portfolio* will be available in April 2016. Please find additional information for your review at mykeyplans.com.

Thank you for your interest in *My Transition Portfolio* and your time in previewing the enclosed copy.

All the best,

Barb Blakeslee
Author, Special Education Teacher
MyKey Consulting Services, LLC
barb@mykeyplans.com

Enclosure

This portfolio belongs to:

_____

Book Publishers Network
P.O. Box 2256
Bothell • WA • 98041
Ph • 425-483-3040
www.bookpublishersnetwork.com

10 9 8 7 6 5 4 3 2 1

Printed in the United States of America

LCCN   2015946887
ISBN   978-1-940598-78-9

Editor: Megan Munroe-Johnson
Cover Designer: Pilar Dowell Designs
Book Designer: Melissa Vail Coffman

Contents

Preface

Barb Blakeslee received her Masters Degree in Special Education in 1995 at Lewis and Clark College in Portland, Oregon. Throughout her career, she has enjoyed on-going education and professional development in the areas of supported employment, technology-based instruction and communication disorders. These three areas have given her a deeply enriched foundation for her career. Much of her time has been spent developing programs for students who are in their transition years and need the programming to support post-school objectives. She has continually pursued best practices in the field of special education and has achieved National Board Certification in the area of Special Education: Exceptional Needs Specialist: Mild/Moderate Disabilities.

A Note from the Author:

Welcome to the *My Transition Portfolio*! I'm so glad you are here. It means that you are either pursuing or supporting meaningful transition, and that you are focused on self-determination strategies. Such a valuable journey!

I began the process of creating this planning guide immediately after a hometown visit with my childhood friend, Laurie Johnson. After 20 years of serving young adults with disabilities and being passionate about quality transition services, it became a top priority for me to find an improved solution to sharing person-centered information.

This planning guide is dedicated with love and gratitude to my friend Laurie for all that I have learned about her, and because of her.

Laurie's Legacy:

I walked with Laurie's mom into her new employment, without warning her that I was coming. When our eyes met, tears flowed. So good to see my childhood friend! She was in the middle of a difficult transition with her support staff, and she not only had a new place to work, but a new home as well. New roommates, new staff, new recreational opportunities, and a new vocational placement. But, no one really knew her—what she truly likes, wanted, or needed.

Laurie is predominantly nonverbal and relies heavily on her parents to communicate her true preferences, throughout her life. Her loving family members are her best advocates and have tirelessly worked with many staff members while weathering a substantial amount of turnover through the years.

Her case manager (who thankfully has known her for many years) was available during my visit, and I informally interviewed her about the transfer of information to Laurie's new support team. She answered key questions while holding a ten-inch stack of files that she was frantically trying to share with Laurie's new caregivers. She made this critical statement, "I just wish there was an easier way to help Laurie communicate the things that make her happy, comfortable, understood, and most of all . . . less anxious. I think her obvious level of frustration would decrease dramatically."

The *My Transition Portfolio* exists to help ease the burden of information-sharing and provides an opportunity for self-determination so that these individuals are known and understood from **their** unique perspective. It is designed for all young adults with disabilities, from highly independent to those who are strongly supported by caregivers.

It's my sincere hope that young adults with disabilities will realize their greatest independence by making their own preferences known with the help of this guide. Wherever necessary, teachers and caregivers can assist them by providing insightful information critical to positive transition planning and successful post-school outcomes.

Thanks to Laurie, I am continually driven to encourage others toward self-determination. I want to stay focused on well-planned, attainable dreams . . . to listen and learn, support and guide.

A small portion of this workbook are duplicated forms, added to the appendix and perforated. It is my intention that the user be allowed to photocopy only these pages (while honoring all other stated copyright protections) and utilize the content as often as necessary.

—Barb Blakeslee

My Transition Portfolio

"Instructions by Max"

My Transition Portfolio and CCSS: Purpose and Process

The Individuals with Disabilities Education Act (IDEA) of 1997, which was upheld in the 2004 re-authorization, mandates that schools provide access to the general education curriculum for all students receiving special education services. The *My Transition Portfolio* is created to support people with disabilities, and all who serve children with severe and multiple disabilities in conceptualizing, planning and implementing activities that involve functional curriculum. The student portfolio development intends to be aligned to Common Core State Standards (CCSS) to the fullest extent possible.

Sample Functional Curriculum Domain Activities are not meant to be inclusive and only address language arts and math strands as outlined by CCSS. Educators are encouraged to utilize the activities in this portfolio as supplemental materials within secondary special education settings.

Language Arts Strands
1. Writing
2. Reading
3. Listening, Speaking and Viewing

Mathematics Strands
1. Number Sense, Properties and Operations
2. Measurement

This portfolio includes selected student learning expectations directly from the CCSS frameworks and uses a matrix visual organizer to provide several sample activities that demonstrate alignment with functional domains. Activities in this portfolio can be merged into classroom and community-based life skills domains to organize instructional efforts such as community, domestic, recreation/leisure and vocational skill areas.

Although this publication is not intended for generating specific test item activities for Alternate Assessments or Portfolio Systems for Students with Disabilities, it is expected to provide educators with a process for determining alignment between models of education that traditionally have been to some extent separate.

These activities are available for use as a starting point for continued classroom discussions and lessons. The educator can then individualize and develop specific activities that align with the education program, demonstrate performance of skills, and document educational opportunities. The author of the *My Transition Portfolio* designed this workbook to be used as an systematic approach for students, with aid from others, to share their personal and critical information with service providers throughout the transition process.

My Transition Portfolio
Common Core State Standards (CCSS) Alignment Examples

Note: Each of the steps #1-12 are aligned and guided to College Career Readiness Anchor Standards (CCR) This is to support a meaningful connection of content standard and transition service support.

Key #1: MyDream - CCR #6: Use technology, including the Internet, to produce/publish writing and to interact and collaborate

CCSS Grade-Level Academic Standard	CCSS Standard - Functional Skill	My Portfolio Articulating Activity
W.11-12.3 Text Types and Purposes	W.3,4,5 With support, produce writing	MyDream Statement
W.11-12.6 CCR: Use of technology	W.3.6 Production/Distribution of Writing	MyDream Statement Poster Project

Key #2: MyStory — CCR #3: Write narratives to develop real or imagined experiences or events using effective techniques

CCSS Grade-Level Academic Standard	CCSS Standard - Functional Skill	My Portfolio Articulating Activity
W.11-12.3 Text Types and Purposes	W.3,4,5 Write narratives to develop real or imagined experiences	MyStory Questionnaire MyStory Narrative
SL.11-12.4 Presentation of knowledge and ideas	SL.3.4 Report on a topic or text, tell a story, or recount an experience	MyStory Narrative: Past, Present, Future

Key #3: MyCommunication — CCR #4: Present information, findings, and supporting evidence such that listeners can follow

CCSS Grade-Level Academic Standard	CCSS Standard - Functional Skill	My Portfolio Articulating Activity
SL.11-12.1 Initiate and participate effectively in a range of collaborative discussions	SL.3.1d Explain their own ideas and understanding in light of discussion	MySpeech Skills: Personal Statement MySocial Solutions
SL.11-12.4 Presentation of knowledge and ideas	SL.3.4 Report on a topic or text, tell a story, or recount an experience with appropriate facts	MyCyber Safety MySocial Solutions MyJournal Entries

Key #4: MySelfie and MyFavorites — CCR #7: Integrate and evaluate presented information in diverse formats and media, including visually and quantitatively, as well as in words.

CCSS Grade-Level Academic Standard	CCSS Standard - Functional Skill	My Portfolio Articulating Activity
RI.11-12.7 Integration of knowledge and ideas	RI.3.7 Use information gained from illustrations (e.g. maps, photographs)	MySelfie and MyFavorites (Photographs) MyPlaces (Maps)
W.11-12.7 Research to build and present knowledge	W.3.7 Conduct short research projects that build knowledge about a topic	MyEvents MyPlaces

Key #5: MySelf Assessments — CCR #5: Develop and strengthen writing as needed by planning revising, editing rewriting or trying a new approach.

CCSS Grade-Level Academic Standard	CCSS Standard - Functional Skill	My Portfolio Articulating Activity
W.11-12.5 Production and distribution of writing	W.3.5 Develop and strengthen writing by planning, revising and editing.	MySelf Assessment MyStrengths Brainstorm Chart, Webs
SL.11-12.2 Comprehension/Collaboration	SL.3.2 Determine main ideas, supporting details	MySelf Assessment MyStrengths Brainstorm Chart, Webs

Key #6: MyCareer Research — CCR #4: Present information, findings, and supporting evidence appropriate to task, purpose, and audience.

CCSS Grade-Level Academic Standard	CCSS Standard - Functional Skill	My Portfolio Articulating Activity
SL.11-12.4 Presentation of knowledge and ideas	SL.3.4 Report on a topic or text	MyCareer Research Planning Web MyCareer Research Essay
W.11-12.6 Use technology including internet to produce, publish and update individual writing products	W.3.6 Use technology to produce writing	MyCareer Research MyResume Development MyPocket Resume

Key #7: MyTransition Plan – CCR #4: Present information, findings, and supporting evidence such that listeners can follow the line of reasoning and the organization, development, and style are appropriate to task, purpose and audience.

CCSS Grade-Level Academic Standard	CCSS Standard - Functional Skill	My Portfolio Articulating Activity
SL.11-12.5 Make Strategic Use of Digital Media	SL.3.4 Report on a topic or text	MyTransition Plan Scavenger Hunt
W.11-12.5 Develop and strengthen writing as needed by planning revising and editing	W.3.5 Develop and strengthen writing as needed by planning, revising and editing	MyTransition Plan MyTransition Plan Essay

Key #8: MyIEP and Transcripts – CCR #4: Present information, findings, and supporting evidence such that listeners can follow the line of reasoning and the organization, development, and style are appropriate to task, purpose and audience.

CCSS Grade-Level Academic Standard	CCSS Standard - Functional Skill	My Portfolio Articulating Activity
SL.11-12.4 Present Information, … conveying clear and distinct perspective such that listeners can follow the line of reasoning	SL.3.4 Report on a topic or text, tell a story, or recount an experience with appropriate facts and relevant details	MyIEP MyStudent-Led IEP MyTranscripts

Key #9: MyCulminating Project – CCR #5: Make strategic use of digital media and visual displays of data to express informationand enhance understanding of presentations.

CCSS Grade-Level Academic Standard	CCSS Standard - Functional Skill	My Portfolio Articulating Activity
SL.11-12.5 Make strategic use of digital media	SL. 3.5 Create engaging audio recordings/add visual displays	MyCulminating Project iMovie Project – MyScripts
W.11-12.6 Use of technology including internet to produce, publish and update	W.L. 3.6 With guidance and support from adults, use technology to produce	MyCulminating Project

Key #10: MyGraduation and Adult Life — CCR #10, 5: Write routinely over extended timeframes. Develop and strengthen writing as needed by planning, revising, editing, rewriting, or trying a new approach.

CCSS Grade-Level Academic Standard	CCSS Standard - Functional Skill	My Portfolio Articulating Activity
W.11-12.10 Range of writing – Write for extended timeframes (time for research, reflection)	W.3.10 Write routinely – for a range of discipline-specific tasks/purposes/audiences.	MyTransition and Adult Life (Reflection)
W.11-12.5 Production and distribution of writing. Develop and strengthen writing as needed by planning revising, editing, rewriting, or trying a new approach.	W.3.5 With guidance and support from peers and adults, develop and strengthen writing as needed by planning, revising, and editing.	MyTransition and Adult Life (Extended into post-high school)

Key #11: MyWork Information — CCR #6: Adapt speech to a variety of contexts and communicative tasks, demonstrating command of formal English when indicated or appropriate.

CCSS Grade-Level Academic Standard	CCSS Standard - Functional Skill	My Portfolio Articulating Activity
SL.11-12.6 Presentation of knowledge and Ideas. Adapt speech to a variety of contexts and communicative tasks, demonstrating command of formal English when indicated or appropriate.	SL.3.6 Speak in complete sentences when appropriate to task and situation in order to provide requested detail or clarification.	MyCo-Workers – "Conversation Starters" requesting help and reporting absenses.

Key #12: MyAdult Service Agencies — CCR #3 Evaluate a speaker's point of view, reasoning, and use of evidence and rhetoric.

CCSS Grade-Level Academic Standard	CCSS Standard - Functional Skill	My Portfolio Articulating Activity
SL.11-12.3 Evaluate a speaker's point of view, reasoning, and use of evidence and rhetoric. Assessing stance, premises, links among ideas.	SL.3.3 Comprehension and collaboration – Ask and answer questions.	MyAgency Notes MyAgency Experiences – Personnel collaboration

Note to Teacher/Caregiver:

It is a top priority of author Barb Blakeslee and MyKey™ Consulting Services, LLC that teaching teams/caregivers understand the importance of using this guide to supplement IEP/transition services in a way that reflects their access to general education standards (IDEA 34 CFR §300.4 Act, 2004). It is encouraged that the student support providers make careful consideration as to how these activities are connected to the Common Core State Standards (CCSS), and allow for students to use self-determination strategies in moving them toward reaching state standards in general education.

This author endeavors to provide a systematic approach for educators in order to make use of best practice in their own classrooms. To that end, thoughtful alignment of functional and vocational skills were made to reach the standards at the 11-12 grade levels as well as college and career readiness (CCR) with specific functional skills highlighted at earlier development stages (i.e., Grade Level 3).

Source:
- National Governors Association Center for Best Practices & Council of Chief State School Officers. (2010). *Common Core State Standards*. Washington, DC: Authors.
- Corestandards.org, Common Core State Standards Initiative

My Personal Information

A Person-Centered Profile

MyPersonal Information Form

All about me!

· ·

❑ **Student Number:** (School ID/State ID #) _____

❑ **Social Security Number:** (Please keep this information confidential. If you are not ready to input this and keep it secure, just write "N/A" for now.) _____ – _____ – _____

❑ **Last Name:** _____

❑ **First Name:** _____

❑ **Middle Name:** _____

❑ **Gender:** (Male or Female?) _____

❑ **Birthdate:** (mm/dd/yyyy) _____

❑ **Phone Number:** _____

❑ **Home Address:**

_____

_____

❑ **Grade in school:** _____

❑ **Age:** _____

❑ **Parent or Guardian's Name(s):** _____

❑ **My Email Address:** _____

❑ **Parent/Caregiver's Email Address:** _____

MyCare Plans and Medical Information

This is your KEY to emergency contacts. Fill this out in case something happens to you and you need medical attention.

Name (Write down your given name.)

First	Last	Nickname

My Phone Number

###	###	####

Gender

☐ Male   ☐ Female

Are you a male (boy) or female (girl)?

Date of Birth

MM	DD	YYYY

Emergency Contact

Please share any contact information that would be helpful in an emergency situation.

1st Contact Person (This should be someone who knows a lot about you personally. This is the first person who should be called or contacted in an emergency situation.)

First	Last

Address (What is this person's address?)

Street Address

City	State / Province / Region

Postal / Zip Code

Home Phone

###	###	####

Cell Phone

###	###	####

2nd Contact Person* (Is there another family member or friend who you would want to contact in case of emergency? This is the second person who should be called or contacted in an emergency situation.)

First   Last

Address (What is this person's address?)

Street Address

City   State / Province / Region

Postal / Zip Code

Home Phone

[   ] – [   ] – [   ]
####

Cell Phone

[   ] – [   ] – [   ]
####

Medical Information

Please share any important medical information that should be known in an emergency situation.

Add a copy of your Permission To Treat form to your Notebook.(Please attach a signed copy of your Permission to Treat form—As needed.)

Who is your primary doctor?

Hospital / Clinic Preference (If you are taken to the hospital, which one would be preferred?)

Medical Insurance Company Name (What is the name of your medical insurance company?)

Insurance Company Phone Number (This should be on the back of your card.)

[   ] – [   ] – [   ]
####

Allergies / Special Health Considerations

[blank box]

- *Are there some foods that you should avoid?*
- *Plants?*
- *Medications?*

Please detail the information that is important to know about you in an emergency situation:

[blank box]

What would someone need to know, if they have never met you?
- *Calming techniques*
- *Specialty equipment*
- *If/Then statements for any given scenario*

Are there specific people who you want or do not want in an emergency situation?

[blank box]

Explain this situation to the best of your ability. Emergency situations should be handled with great care and consideration.
- *Who do you want around in an emergency?*
- *Who do you prefer to have at a distance in an emergency?*

MyFood and Nutrition

Share some information about your favorite foods and nutrition choices.

Name

First	Last

Date

| MM | / | DD | / | YYYY |

Food Allergies

Are there any foods that you are allergic to?
- *Please describe with as much detail as possible.*

Dietary Restrictions

Has a doctor put you on any sort of nutrition plan?

Are there some foods that you simply should avoid?

What is your typical daily water intake? (How much water do you think you drink in a typical day?)

Do you drink any of the following? (Drinks high in caffeine or sugar should be taken in moderation.)
❏ Coffee
❏ Tea
❏ Energy drinks
❏ Alcohol
❏ Soda

MyMeals

Describe some of you favorite foods.

How often do you eat in a day? (You can keep a food journal and track your eating for a few days or a week to get a good idea.)

What are some of your favorite BREAKFAST foods?

If you were to have the greatest breakfast, what would it be?

What are some of your favorite things to eat for LUNCH?

If you were to have the greatest lunch, what would it be?

Do you like to eat snacks? What kind?

Do you like:
- *Chips?*
- *Crackers?*
- *Healthy snacks?*

What are some of your favorite things to have for DINNER?

If you were to have the greatest dinner, what would it be?

What are some of your favorite things to have for DESSERT?

What are some desserts that you really love?
- *Ice cream?*
- *Cake?*
- *Cookies?*
- *Fruit?*

What are some of your favorite VEGETABLES?

❑ Broccoli   ❑ Carrots   ❑ Onions
❑ Kale   ❑ Peas   ❑ Corn
❑ Spinach   ❑ Tomatoes   ❑ Brussels Sprouts
❑ Asparagus   ❑ Bell Peppers   ❑ Zucchini
❑ Green Beans   ❑ Cauliflower   ❑ Avocado

What are some of your favorite FRUITS?

❑ Blueberries   ❑ Apples   ❑ Bananas
❑ Oranges   ❑ Cantaloupe   ❑ Kiwi
❑ Grapes   ❑ Strawberries   ❑ Grapefruit
❑ Pineapple   ❑ Watermelon   ❑ Pears
❑ Peaches   ❑ Nectarines   ❑ Raspberries

Are you on any special diets? Please describe:

Are you on any of the following:
- *Gluten free*
- *Casein free*
- *Dairy free*
- *Sugar/artificial sweetener free*

Write out or attach a copy of your nutrition plan to your Transition Notebook.

MyHealth Information

Use this form to gather and share information about your personal health.

. . . .

Name

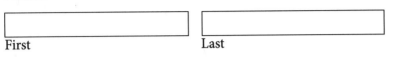

First   Last

Date

MM   DD   YYYY

. . . .

About My Health

Share as much information about your health as you would like.

I generally feel...

❑ Healthy
❑ Healthy most of the time
❑ Sick sometimes
❑ Sick much of the time

Tell about your health status when you were a baby.

Refer back to parents/caregivers who can tell about your health status when you were young.

Take a look at medical reports from your younger years.

What is the most stressful thing in your life right now?

This could be anything that makes you feel:
- *Angry*
- *Anxious*
- *Worried*
- *Fearful*
- *Nervous*

What are some past health considerations that you would want people to know about?

What is your current health care plan?

What is your current health care plan?

Are there some specific health regimens or schedules that people should know about your current health care and any concerns?

Add a copy of your Emergency Care Plan to your Notebook.

If you can, add a copy of your medication to your Notebook as well.

Are you experiencing any pain currently? (This is an opportunity to share any concerns that you might have about your body and your health. Check all that apply.)

- ❑ Stomach Pain
- ❑ Pain in Arms
- ❑ Pain in Joints
- ❑ Headaches
- ❑ Dizziness
- ❑ Shortness of Breath
- ❑ Constipation or Diarrhea

- ❑ Back Pain
- ❑ Pain in Legs
- ❑ Problems with Periods
- ❑ Pain in Chest
- ❑ Heart Pounding or Racing
- ❑ Nausea
- ❑ Other: _____

Any additional information that you would like to share about your personal health?

Please work with your parent or caregiver to provide any necessary information regarding your healthcare and protection.

MyWorkout Survey

Fill this in to tell people about your fitness interests.

Add a picture of your favorite exercises to your Notebook. (You can find workout ideas and routines on the Internet or from a physical therapist.)

Add a "Before Workout Program" picture to your Notebook. (This should be an socially appropriate picture of yourself before you started your workout program.)

Add an "After Workout Program" picture to your Notebook. (When you complete a goal or a workout program, attach a picture of your changed self!)

Name

First	Last

Date

	/	/
MM	DD	YYYY

What is your gender?
❑ Male
❑ Female

What is your age?

What is your height?

What is your weight?

Have you ever smoked cigarettes?
❑ Yes
❑ No

Do you regularly engage in any of the following exercises?

☐ Walking ☐ Running ☐ Swimming ☐ Biking ☐ Other ☐ I don't exercise.

If you walk for exercise, on average, how long does it take you to walk one mile?

[   ] (Leave blank if you do not walk for exercise.)

If you run for exercise, on average, how long does it take you to run one mile?

[   ] (Leave blank if you do not run for exercise.)

If you bicycle for exercise, on average, how long is your normal ride?

[   ] (Leave blank if you do not ride a bicycle for exercise.)

On average, how many hours a week do you exercise?

[   ] (This is just a rough estimate of the amount of hours/week in the past few weeks.)

On average, how many hours a night do you sleep?

[   ] (This is just a rough estimate of the amount of hours/night in the past few weeks.)

Add items to your Transition Notebook

Add a copy of your proposed workout program to your Notebook. (You can find sample workout plans online or you can create one for yourself.)

Make a list of some people you would want to workout with:

[   ]

You could think of some:
- *Family?*
- *Friends?*
- *Co-workers?*

Write your workout goals here: (Example: By _____ I would like to be able to _____ and decrease/increase my _____ by _____.)

[   ]

What would you like to work on stengthening?

What are some new workouts that you would like to do?
- *Crossfit?*
- *Aerobics?*
- *Sport specific exercise?*
- *Dance routines?*

MySchedule

This documents your daily schedule. Structure your day so that you take steps toward a productive and fun life.

. . . .

Name

First   Last

Date

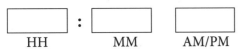

MM   DD   YYYY

. . . .

Getting Up and Getting Ready

What do you do from the time you wake up in the morning?

Wake Up:

HH   :   MM   AM/PM

Breakfast Time

HH   :   MM   AM/PM

Description of Activity: (What are some things that you need to do to get ready for your day?)

Description of Activity:

Description of Activity:

Get Going: (What time do you need to leave or catch your bus?)

HH   :   MM   AM/PM

My School/Work Schedule

What does your schedule look like when you are hard at work?

Arrival Time: (What time do you need to be at work, school or program?)

	:		
HH		MM	AM/PM

Description of MyActivity at Work or School: (In this section list several activities that you typically do in your daily routine.)

Another Description of MyActivity at Work or School: (Are there preferred activities you would like people to know about?)

I also...

Then, I...

Lastly, another activity or task is:

Lunch Time

	:		
HH		MM	AM/PM

Add items to your Transition Notebook

Detailed Work/School Schedule Attachment (Add a copy of your specific work schedule for the day, week or month to your Notebook.)

Recreation/Leisure Time

Schedule some time for relaxing, hobbies or working out.

Leisure, Event or Game Time (What time do you want to be set aside for some leisure time?)

HH	MM	AM/PM

Description of Activity: (What do you do for fun? Something that you really look forward to? Something that is very rewarding in your day?)

Time

HH	MM	AM/PM

Description of Activity:

• •

Evening Activities

How do you like to wind it down at night?

Dinner Time (What time do you expect to have dinner?)

HH	MM	AM/PM

Description of Activity: (What are some activities that you need to do in the evening time?)

Description of Activity:

Description of Activity:

Bed Time

HH	MM	AM/PM

Add items to your Transition Notebook

Daily Schedule Attachment (Add a copy of your individualized schedule to your Notebook)

Additional comments about your personal schedule:

Key #1:
"Develop Your Dream"

MyDream

The Main Key Belief: A Note to Teachers and Caregivers

Dreaming about the future's possibilities brings hope. Walking with a person who has a disability through the process of developing their own attainable dream gives a sense of purpose and meaning while supporting self-discovery within each person's unique giftedness.

Providing a systematic discovery process where these individuals can become advocates for themselves is central to finding successful independent living outcomes. A thoughtful system can also provide an incredible opportunity for the individual, caregivers and community members to communicate more effectively and celebrate the strengths of that individual.

A Case for the Cause

Several years ago, I had the opportunity to lead a student toward her real dream as she focused and built upon her strengths. Ashley was a student with autism in my high school classroom. She was an incredible representation of joy, a very hard worker, and had a personality that quickly engaged others. She specifically had a deep appreciation for Disney as she related anything and everything to the Magical Kingdom.

Ashley could turn the most mundane situations or conversation into a delightful exchange that linked Mickey or Minnie in the cleverest of ways. When asked what she wanted to do after high school, she was clear on her answer: "I want to go to Disney University, work at Disneyworld and live at Disney's Town of Celebration." Ashley's family was on board with this dream of hers, and if given the chance, were willing to move across the country to see her fulfill her dream. However, with other kids in the family and a job that made it next to impossible to relocate, she was left to explore other avenues to fulfill her interests and capitalize on other skill areas.

Being quite proficient in maintaining order and following structured activities, Ashley showed promise for a variety of work experiences within her community. After completing high school, she participated in the 18-21 transition program offered by her school district's special education department.

One year post-graduation for Ashley, I shifted my work with the high school students in a class setting to an adult transition program where students could continue working toward goals in their individualized education plan. I was able to have Ashley once again on my caseload and was excited to continue on with her educational growth now in community-based instruction.

As predicted, Ashley was participating with enthusiasm in a variety of community work experiences and social activities which added to her resume and continued to hone her skills in organization and social development. During her three years of participation in the transition program, she never let go of her dream to work at Disney. Her parents found her a seasonal position at the Disney Store in the mall which lasted for a short time and resulted in a satisfying volunteer position.

Along the path toward employment, there were many who doubted that Ashley would achieve the dream she had for herself but she always maintained her focus. There was much information gathered to guide her teams in supporting her goals. A great deal of evaluation data had been collected, and the staff around her developed a substantial vocational portfolio.

In Ashley's last year, she took the challenge of participating in a very unique partnership between the school district, vocational rehabilitation, the local developmental disabilities administration, and Seattle Children's Hospital.

During that time of internship and discovery at Children's Hospital, there were several different vocational training opportunities explored, each for ten weeks at time. With no surprise, Ashley became well liked and was a very reliable and productive worker. Late in her discovery process while in her fourth internship at the hospital as a Child Life Specialist Assistant, Ashley encountered her most coveted cast member coming toward her, down a long corridor—Mickey Mouse! Ashley gasped and let out the most authentic burst of joy, and exclaimed, "Mickey! I've finally found you. It's me, Ashley!"

That day was the start of a great partnership where she would work beside Mickey and Minnie in addition to other "cast members" to bring cheer, interpersonal connection, joy, and hope to children needing some relief and diversion from their medical treatments. Ashley would use her organizational skills and good memory to keep craft closets organized and set up games for patients. The staff, patients, and families loved her contribution to the department so much that they offered her a 30-hour per week position at a great hourly rate!

Several years later, Ashley remains employed in the same position, but has expanded her responsibilities. She rides the public bus an hour and a half each way and is experiencing great independence. When asked about her feelings about her job and if she intended to continue, she responded with just as much enthusiasm as she had when first started: "Why, yes! I get to work with Mickey and Minnie all the time and the children are so cute!"

There is no doubt that given the chance to work at Disneyworld, Ashley would jump at the opportunity. However, the experience she has had in a job that approximates her dream allows her to enjoy using the skills that she naturally possesses. She shines as an individual in the Child Life Program, and although job security is not guaranteed for her, it is a reasonable expectation of continued employment and social connections.

An Attainable Outcome

When a person like Ashley is allowed to participate and take ownership in their own goal setting, based upon data from a formalized vocational evaluation, attainable outcomes are far more likely to occur. These individuals are then able to take more independent, authentic steps toward attainable outcomes.

Ultimately, an increased sense of purpose and meaning is compounded with a sense of hope. This happens when a person is allowed to more fully express and experience their unique areas of strength and take an honest look at their areas of weakness.

Oftentimes, students are unsure of the possibilities that are available to them within their own community simply because they are not able to identify their own skill sets. It is an educator or caregiver's role to assist and to guide an individual to opportunities that can capitalize on strengths and weaknesses without compromising or discounting the person's "big dream."

This following "MyDream Statement" section allows the user the opportunity to be guided through a process to identify the attainable dream they have for themselves. The prompts should assist the user and/ or their caregivers in connecting to truly person-centered information sharing.

MyDream Statement

Please fill out this form to tell about yourself - your hopes and dreams!

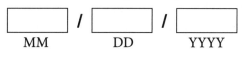

Name (Write your name, and let people know who you are! Nice to meet you. :)

First	Last

Date (What is today's date?)

[   ] / [   ] / [   ]
MM   DD   YYYY

Dreams and Skills

Often your "MyDream Statement" is best developed when you are able to use your personal skills and abilities.
Go ahead...write about what you consider to be your best skill.

What would you consider to be your "BEST SKILL?" (Something you are really good at)

This could be something like...
- *Artistic: great at drawing.*
- *People skills: I get along with people well.*
- *Technology: Great with computers, etc.*

If you could choose any job USING THIS SKILL, what would it be?

This should be a job that...
- *You have the education to do.*
- *You could get an education to do.*
- *You could access independently or carpool to get there.*

Check off some things that you would need to do or work on (improve) in order to do the job stated. These are the things that are necessary for you to reach the dream you have for yourself:

- ❏ Drive a car
- ❏ Live on an accessible bus line
- ❏ Increase my skill level in certain areas
- ❏ Obtain a certification
- ❏ Get a college degree
- ❏ Take specific high school classes
- ❏ Increase my attendance in school
- ❏ Finish assigned tasks
- ❏ Learn how to follow schedules really well

- ❏ Work on improving hygiene and self-care
- ❏ Increase respect for others
- ❏ Learn and apply good self-monitoring techniques
- ❏ Increase reading skills
- ❏ Increase writing skills
- ❏ Use my communication system effectively
- ❏ Work on memory and recall
- ❏ Increase ability to take constructive criticism

What are some additional things that you might need to know or be able to do in order to do that job?

<table>
<tr><td></td></tr>
</table>

Are there some things that you know you might need, but aren't listed above?

Particular skills?

· ·

Write about some of the dreams you have for your own life!

"MyDream" should be centered on whatever makes you the happiest. What is that for you?

Add items to your Transition Notebook

Add a PICTURE of yourself, and/or something about your "Dream" to your Notebook. (Find a picture that will show people your personality, preferences and dream.)

Tell about something you do that makes you the HAPPIEST.

<table>
<tr><td></td></tr>
</table>

Are you happiest when you are:
- *With people you love?*
- *Quietly doing artwork?*
- *Playing Sports?*
- *At work, using your skills?*
- *At home, doing something enjoyable?*
- *Listening to music or playing an instrument?*

Where do you see yourself LIVING in the future?

Would you like to live...
- *In some beautiful place?*
- *A specific living situation?*
- *In another country, state or city?*

Where could you WORK in your own community in the future?

Would you like to work at...
- *A place where you interact with others*
- *Use your own hobby, interests, knowledge or skills?*

How much MONEY would you like to make at this job per HOUR? (You can find this information online. Check your career center for great web sources.)

$ [   ] . [   ]
Dollars   Cents

How much MONEY would you like to make at this job per MONTH? (You can find this information online. Multiply the hourly rate by the number of hours you expect to work per week. Then, multiply by the number of weeks in a month.)

$ [   ] . [   ]
Dollars   Cents

Who could you talk to about the dream you have for yourself?

Would you want to talk to...
- *A parent?*
- *A teacher?*
- *Your case manager?*

MyDream Statement

Given the information you added above, write a "MyDream Statement" for yourself.

MyDream Statement - A Paragraph About Me

Example: The dream I have for myself is to be as _____ as possible. In my life, I really want to work at _____ and live in _____. I really feel like I would be the happiest if I could _____.

Use this space to brainstorm more about your "MyDream Statement." (What are the things that you really want?)

MyDream Statement
Poster Project Task List

1. ❑ Get your hands on your MyDream Statement form.

2. ❑ Brainstorm some ideas you have for your life after graduation.

3. ❑ Discuss your plans with one or two partners.

4. ❑ Check errors . . . and discuss completion with teacher.

5. ❑ Grab a pen or highlighter!

6. ❑ Circle **key words** you have written about your own dreams.

7. ❑ Talk through your "key words" with a <u>peer or adult</u>.

8. ❑ Match **key words** with pictures found in magazines or online.

9. ❑ Fill pages with your pictures showing MyDream images in a Word Document or other computer application.

10. ❑ Share finished "Images Document" with teacher for review.

11. ❑ Have teacher re-size pictures to fit on poster – print copies.

12. ❑ Cut out pictures out for your poster project.

13. ❑ Get a blank poster board.

14. ❑ Get color pencils.

15. ❑ In big bubble letters, draw your name at the top.

16. ❑ Write categories on poster board in sections.

17. ❑ Add pictures to poster with glue.

18. ❑ Add captions to each picture.

19. ❑ Decorate with a lot of color!

20. ❑ Report completion to teacher or turn in assignment.

Materials Needed:
- Poster Board
- Pens
- Color Pencils
- Highlighter
- Scissors
- Glue

Key #2:
"Share Your Own Story"

MyStory

MyStory—A Letter to Caregivers

(*See Appendix for perforated copy and send home with the MyStory Questionnaire*)

Student Name: _____

Date: _____

Dear Parents/Guardians:

In the next few weeks, our class will begin a unit called "MyStory." In this unit, we will be working with students to assist them in telling the story about their life's journey so far. We will be highlighting events from their early childhood and infants/toddlers, school years and young-adult experiences. The information gathered in this process will then be shared through essay writing and in opportunities to give voice to their own life experiences.

We have provided students a questionnaire which contains prompts to guide their thoughts as they reflect on specific information that they want to share. It is our hope that you will be able to assist your student at home in recalling those experiences and that we will be able to build on individual stories in the classroom setting. We see this opportunity as a shared experience between the staff, students, and caregivers, but want to ensure that our students are able to independently communicate their own perspectives and deliver the information in whatever way works best for them and their communication style.

Please see the attached questionnaire and follow the prompts with your student as their homework assignment. We are excited to hear about any of the details from their personal history and will make sure that we keep any information confidential if so indicated by you. Thank you in advance for your participation in creating a rich and valuable perspective on the life of your student. This information will be kept in their developing portfolio and the final copy of their written essay will be sent home.

Please indicate below any information that you would like to share or anything that you would prefer to keep confidential.

All the best!

Information from Parent/Guardian:

MyStory Questionnaire
Assisted by Parent/Caregiver

(*See Appendix for perforated copy*)

Use this fillable form to gather information about your life: Past, Present, and Future. You will have an opportunity to use this information in your "All About Me" narrative.

• •

Name

|_____| |_____|
First   Last

Date

|_____| / |_____| / |_____|
MM   DD   YYYY

• •

Early Childhood Years...

Where were you born?

- *What was the hospital name?*
- *What city/state?*
- *What were the other conditions on the day your were born?*

| |
| |
| |
| |
| |
| |

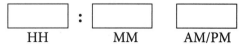

Add a map of the place you were born to your Notebook. (You can use a web-based map to show where you were born or raised. Attach your printed map or picture of where you were born.)

When were you born? (Do you know the exact time you were born?)

|_____| : |_____| |_____|
HH   MM   AM/PM

What were you like as a baby?

> - *What do you see from pictures or hear about yourself from parents/caregivers?*
> - *What was your personality like?*

Add a baby picture to your Notebook! People will love seeing this.

What were your favorite things as a baby?

> *Favorite toys?*

Add a picture of your favorite toy to your Notebook.
(You were no doubt adorable!!!)

. . . .

Elementary School Years...

Describe what you remember about pre-school and elementary school here.

Did you go to a pre-school? If so, where?

What elementary school did you go to? (Do you remember the name of the school?)

What do you remember about elementary school?

- *Best friends?*
- *Favorite games/toys?*
- *Teachers?*

Add an elementary school picture to share and remember where you went to school to your Notebook.

Junior High Years...

What was the name of your junior high or middle school?

What was your favorite thing about junior high school? ...and least favorite?

Junior high school can be very difficult, but it can also be very fun.

What are your memories from that time?

Did you have a favorite teacher?

- *Who was the teacher? Why were they your favorite?*
- *What did they help you to do or learn?*
- *Have you ever stayed in contact with them?*
- *Is there anything else you can add?*

Favorite subject in junior high:

- *Math*
- *English*
- *PE*
- *Art*
- *Social Studies*

MyTransition from junior high to high school:

Describe your experiences moving from junior high to high school.

Were you…Nervous? Scared? Excited? Happy?

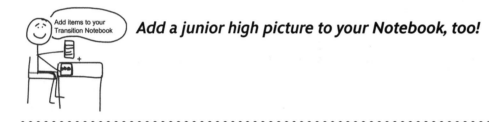 **Add a junior high picture to your Notebook, too!**

High School Years

What high school did you go to?

What was your sophomore year like?

- *Classes*
- *Teachers*
- *Friends*
- *Sports*

What was your junior year like? Or, what do you hope it will be like?

- *Classes*
- *Teachers*
- *Friends*
- *Sports*
- *Clubs*

What was your senior year like? Or, what do you hope it will be like?

- *Classes*
- *Teachers*
- *Friends*
- *Sports*
- *Graduation planning*

Add items to your Transition Notebook

Add a picture from high school to your Notebook...this could be a dance, sports or the school itself.

- -

MyFuture Goals

Write about two goals you have for the future here.

What would you like to have happen in your life?

Are there some things that you would like to change?

(Brainstorm Here)

Goal #1 (Write your goal titles or domain areas here.)

Goal #2

Use this example if you would like!

Example:
By _____, I would like to be able to _____.
In the future, I would also really like to _____

MyStory – Narrative

Use the information gathered from your MyStory Questionnaire to write about your life's journey. Describe your past, present and future goals. This will help you tell your own story.

• •

Name

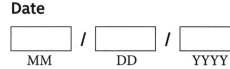

First   Last

Date

[ ] / [ ] / [ ]

MM   DD   YYYY

• •

Your Personal Introduction - Practice Paragraph

Write an introduction for yourself
- *What is your full name?*
- *How old are you?*
- *What grade are you in? (If still in school)*
- *What are some important things about you in general?*

Your Past Information - Practice Paragraph

- *What are some significant things about your past?*
- *Where did you grow up?*
- *Write down 3-5 things about your past experiences in life.*

Your Present Situation - Practice Paragraph

Currently, what is your life like?

- *Where do you live?*
- *Who do you live with?*
- *Where do you work?*
- *What do you do in your free-time?*

Your Hopes for the Future - Practice Paragraph

When you think of your future, what are you really looking forward to?

- *This year?*
- *In 1 year?*
- *In 5 years?*
- *In 10 years?*

Your Strengths and Weaknesses - Practice Paragraph

Generally, tell about the things that you are good at, and things that you could work on to be better.

*Refer to the strengths/weaknesses brainstorming chart.

(You will go more in depth with this in "Key 5: MySelf Assessments")

Rough Draft: Use this section to write your rough draft:

Use the information from the paragraphs on the previous pages.

- *Add transition sentences between paragraphs*
- *Fix any spelling errors*
- *Fix grammar errors*
- *Change wording if it is repetitive*

(if applicable)
- *Create a heading*
- *Write your teachers name*
- *Write the date*
- *Write the name of the class you are in*

If you need more space, add a separate page here.

Final Draft of MyStory Essay (Re-write or attach your final draft to your Transition Notebook.)

MyStory – The Basics

Name

First	Last

Date

| MM | / | DD | / | YYYY |

When I was little I was very _____.

My favorite toy was: _____ _____. I really liked to play _____.

When I was little, my favorite food was: _____.

The cartoon I liked the best was: _____.

When I went to school I was good at: _____.

My favorite thing to do on the playground was: _____.

My favorite candy was: _____.

When I got a little older, I have had things that I really like and other things that I don't like so much.

I do/do not like school because _____.

My favorite teacher is _____.

because _____.

My favorite video game is _____ because _____.

The best thing about high school is _____.

The thing I like to do most in my spare time is _____

_____.

My best friend(s) is/are: _____.

I like them because _____.

Some things I can plan to do with my friends in the future are:

First, I could _____

_____.

Another thing I could do with friends is _____

_____.

Lastly, I would do something very different and go to _____

_____.

My life is _____.

I really hope I will get to _____ in the future.

MyPictures

Add some of your favorite pictures from any stage of life with or without other people. Just try to write when the picture was taken. :)

Name

First	Last

Date

[　　] / [　　] / [　　　]
MM　　　DD　　YYYY

 *Add a photo of yourself to your Notebook - #1* (Find a picture on your computer to print and attach to your Notebook Make it a good one. :)

Describe this picture

- *When was it taken?*
- *Who is in the picture?*
- *Where was it taken?*
- *Why is this picture important to you?*

 *Add a photo of yourself to your Notebook- #2* (For the rest of the pictures that you would like to attach to your Notebook, make sure that you tell about them on this page!)

Describe this picture

Continued...

Add a photo of yourself to your Notebook - #3 (If applicable, place pictures in an envelope and paper clip or add them to your Notebook.)

Describe this picture

Add a photo of yourself to your Notebook - #4

Describe this picture

Add a photo of yourself to your Notebook - #5

Describe this picture

 *Add a photo of yourself to your Notebook - #6*

Describe this picture

 *Add a photo of yourself to your Notebook - #7*

Describe this picture

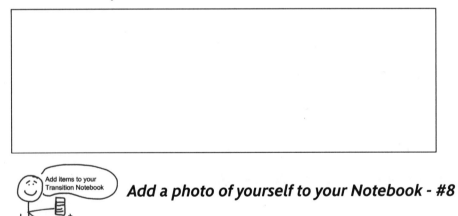 *Add a photo of yourself to your Notebook - #8*

Describe this picture

MyFamily

This is a place where you can show and write
about the people who are in your family.

Family
Me

• •

Name

First	Last

Date

	/	/	
MM	DD	YYYY	

• •

MyFamily

Tell a little about your family relationships

This is a picture of my whole family. (Find a picture of you and your family to add
to your Notebook.):

Who is in this picture? (Picture #1)

This is another picture of my family. (Find a picture of you and your family to add
to your Notebook.)

Who is in this picture? (Picture #2) (Keep adding more if you would like...)

This is yet another picture of my family.

Who is in this picture? (Picture #3)

Add items to your Transition Notebook

This is a picture of my family pet. (Find a picture of your family pet to add to your Notebook. If you have more than one, show them off, too!)

What is the name of your pet(s)?

What language is spoken in your home?

Tell about where your family has lived. (Where are the places you have lived in your life?)

Do you live with your family now? When did you move out? (How do you feel about living away from your family if you don't currently live with them?)

List out the names of the people who are in your family.

1. *Write the names of your family members*
2. *Tell what relation they are to you:*
   - *Mother/Father/Caregiver*
   - *Sister*
   - *Brother*
   - *Aunt*
   - *Uncle*

Tell about a great family memory.

*   *A great trip*
*   *A fun sporting event*
*   *A family reunion*
*   *A funny family story*
*   *A great family meal*

If there was something significant that happened or if you needed help, which family member would you call?

Would you call
*   *Someone you feel most comfortable with?*
*   *Someone who you live closest to?*
*   *Someone who knows you and your information the best?*

What are some traditions that your family has during the holidays?

Tell about some of the things that your family has alway done during the holidays.
*   *Is there somewhere you always go?*
*   *Is there something that they always cook?*
*   *Is there a movie that you always like to watch during holidays?*
*   *Do you usually travel to the same place?*

MyParents

Describe your parents (if applicable):

- What are their names?
- What do they like?
- What do they do?
- Do you live with them?
- How are you like them?

MyBrothers/Sisters

Describe your siblings (if applicable):
- What are their names?
- What do they like?
- What do they do?
- Where do they live?
- How are you like them?

MyGrandparents

Describe your grandparents (if applicable):
- What are their names?
- What do they like?
- What do they do?
- Where do they live?
- How are you like them?

MyCousins

Describe your cousins (if applicable):
- What are their names?
- What do they like?
- What do they do?
- Where do they live?

Attach a copy   **Attach a copy of your family tree here:** (You can create a diagram of your family tree online and then print and attach a copy here if you would like.)

MyFriends

This is a place where you can write about
the people who are your closest friends

· ·

Name

First	Last

Date

	/		/		
MM		DD		YYYY	

· ·

MyFriends

Share some pictures and information about your friends.

Add items to your Transition Notebook

Picture #1 of my friends (Find a picture of you and your friends to add to your Notebook.)

Describe who and what this picture shows!

Picture #2 of my friends (Find another picture of you and your friends to add to your Notebook.)

Describe who and what this picture shows!

Picture #3 of my friends (If you have more pictures that you would like to share, ...do it!)

Describe who and what this picture shows!

Picture #4 of my friends

Describe who and what this picture shows!

Describe how you feel when you are with your closest friends. Why do you think you feel do you think you feel that way?

Friendships often help us to feel great about ourselves. Why do you think you feel...
- *encouraged by your friends?*
- *happy when you are with them?*
- *valued and respected?*
- *more important when you are with them?*
- *like you can laugh with them more than others?*

List out the names of the people who you feel are closest to you and know you the best.

1. Write the names of your closest friends
2. Tell about how and where you met them

Tell about a great memory you have with one or some of your closest friends.

- *A funny event*
- *Something at school*
- *The story about how you met*
- *A time that you laughed really hard with them*

If there was something significant that happened or if you needed help, which friend would you call first?

Would you call...
- *Someone you feel most comfortable with?*
- *Someone who you live closest to?*
- *Someone who knows you and your information the best?*

Making Friends

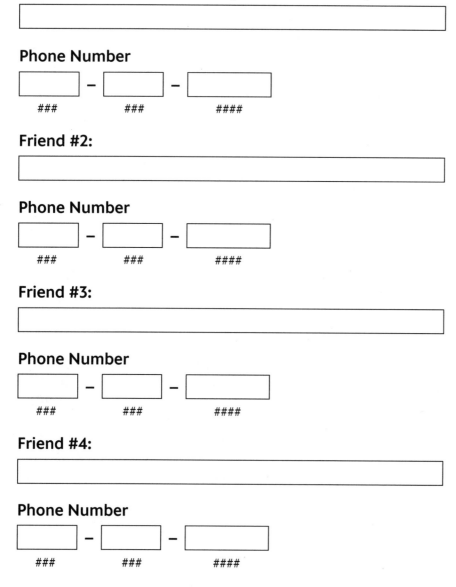

Would you like to make new friends?
- *Where could you meet new people?*
- *Who would you like to get to know?*
- *When could you pursue new friendships?*
- *What events could you invite new friends to?*

Friend #1: (Make a list of some of your friends and their phone numbers here:)

Phone Number

[ ] – [ ] – [ ]

\#\#\#　　　\#\#\#　　　\#\#\#\#

Friend #2:

Phone Number

[ ] – [ ] – [ ]

\#\#\#　　　\#\#\#　　　\#\#\#\#

Friend #3:

Phone Number

[ ] – [ ] – [ ]

\#\#\#　　　\#\#\#　　　\#\#\#\#

Friend #4:

Phone Number

[ ] – [ ] – [ ]

\#\#\#　　　\#\#\#　　　\#\#\#\#

Key #3:
"Tell About Your Communication Style"

MyCommunication

MySpeech Skills

This form is designed to help you tell about the ways that you are understood and heard by others.

. . . .

Name

First		Last

Date

MM	/	DD	/	YYYY

. . . .

Level #1

How comfortable are you using your speech skills to do the following:

I can introduce myself to others. (Can you use speech to say: a greeting, ask for someone's name, make a statement, state your own name, and tell them a closing comment

❑ Yes
❑ No
❑ I can with practice
❑ I prefer that someone else help with this

I can advocate for myself by stating a need and then asking a question. (Can you advocate by yourself by communicating things like: "I am unsure of what to do. Can you help?", "I don't understand the directions. Can you tell me again in a different way?", "I don't know where to go. Can you show me?")

❑ Yes
❑ No
❑ I can with practice
❑ I prefer that someone else help with this

I can ask someone a question about themselves. (Can you ask a question if there is something you'd like to learn? Are you able to ask a question to find out some information?)

❑ Yes
❑ No
❑ I can with practice
❑ I prefer that someone else help with this

I can order a simple meal at a restaurant or school cafeteria. (Are you able to: state a greeting, request an item(s) you would like to eat, and say "Thank you"?)

❑ Yes
❑ No
❑ I can with practice
❑ I prefer that someone else help with this

I can take turns in a conversation with a friend (2-3 turns). (Can you: ask questions, take an appropriate turn when asked a question, comment on partner's shared topic, make additional comments and/or close the conversation?)

❑ Yes
❑ No
❑ I can with practice
❑ I prefer that someone else help with this

I can make a request for information when I need help from someone in the community. (If you need directions or are in need of help (always find a safe person; i.e., police, security, worker): Use a greeting, ask a question to get information, say "Thank you" for helping out).

❑ Yes
❑ No
❑ I can with practice
❑ I prefer that someone else help with this

• •

Level #2

What is your comfort level with more detailed information?

I can handle full conversations about topics that I know about in an organized way. (Think about exchanging information about a topic you know well and would like to discuss with someone else.)

❑ Yes
❑ No
❑ I can with practice
❑ I prefer that someone else help with this

I can talk about information that is not related to my own daily life. (This might be about: your community, social or sporting events, world events, wther current events.)

❑ Yes
❑ No
❑ I can with practice
❑ I prefer that someone else help with this

I feel comfortable interviewing for jobs and can answer questions with confidence. (I can answer questions by the interviewer and offer extended responses.)

❑ Yes
❑ No
❑ I can with practice
❑ I prefer that someone else help with this

I can talk about a trip or some other everyday event that happened in the recent past or that will happen soon. (I can use my long-term memory to discuss the details of an event in my life.)

❑ Yes
❑ No
❑ I can with practice
❑ I prefer that someone else help with this

I can offer my own opinions when they differ from others and defend my own views. (I can formulate my own opinions and explain why I feel the way I do about the things I am saying.)

❑ Yes
❑ No
❑ I can with practice
❑ I prefer that someone else help with this

MySpeech Personal Statement

Take some time to write about how you feel about using your voice to communicate with others.

How would you describe (in detail) your own ability to communicate?

- *Do you feel comfortable talking to others?*
- *How do you feel about sharing your feelings with others?*
- *Do you feel like people listen to you when you talk?*
- *Do you feel comfortable introducing yourself to people you don't know?*
- *Do you feel easily understood?*

Is there anything about your speech that you would like to work on?

Are there some goals that you have... like:

- *Be able to interview for a job*
- *Order for myself in a restaurant*
- *Hold better conversations with friends*
- *Be able to express myself better*

MyCommunication Style

Your easiest and most effective way to communicate with others.

• •

Name

First		Last	

Date

[   ] / [   ] / [   ]
MM   DD   YYYY

• •

Communication Preferences

In general, how do you like to communicate?

How do you like to communicate with your friends?

Texting, phone calls, email? Or, would it be talking, writing notes, using a communication device?

Add items to your Transition Notebook

Add a picture of your best communication device or mode to your Notebook. (This could be a phone, communication device, book, computer, or simply a picture of you talking.)

Tell about a time when you really felt like someone listened to you and understood you.

This could be a situation:
- *At home*
- *In your classroom/school*
- *Telling a friend something important*
- *Telling someone how you like things*

• •

Listening to others

What helps you to take in information and become a great listener?

How do you listen best?

❑ Just tell me things with words
❑ I like things written down
❑ I prefer to be shown or have things drawn in pictures
❑ I like to watch something in a video to understand
❑ I like a combination of talking, writing and drawing

I prefer to have a conversation or interact with...

❑ One person at a time
❑ Just a couple of people at a time
❑ A small group is okay
❑ I like a large group to talk to
❑ I prefer to talk to a lot of people

. . . .

Self Expression

What helps you to communicate with others?

I am best able to communicate with others... (Make a choice to show what best describes your own self-expression.)

❑ Using gestures
❑ Using ASL/sign language
❑ Using some sign and a few words
❑ Combining gestures, drawing, and some words
❑ Using just a few words - talking
❑ Using short sentences - talking
❑ Having short conversations - talking
❑ Having a longer conversation about topics I enjoy
❑ Having long conversations about anything

I can ask someone a question about themselves.

- *Do you have a memorable conversation with a friend?*
- *Who understands you the best?*
- *What should others know about your communication style so that you are better understood?*

MyJournal Entries *(See Appendix for perforated copy)*

Use this space to write some of your thoughts down:

• •

Name

First	Last

Date

	/		/	
MM		DD		YYYY

• •

Describe a current problem here:

What could be a potential solution to this problem or situation?

Journal Entry/Notes   Date: ___/___/_____

Teachers/Caregivers:

Please make copies of this page as needed for additional entries.

Journal Entry/Notes   Date: ___/___/_____

Journal Entry/Notes   Date: ___/___/_____

MySocial Solutions (See Appendix for perforated copy)

Name: _____

Date: _____

The Setting	The Problem (State the conflict...)	The Staff Involved
When? Who was involved? Where? What Happened?	(Name) Felt... Because...	Who was involved?
_____ _____ _____ _____ _____	_____ _____ _____ _____ _____	_____ _____ _____ _____ _____

My Solution (Attempt)	My Outcome • What happened next? • How did the story end?	My Lesson Learned
MyChoice is...	MyConclusion	I now know...
_____ _____ _____ _____	_____ _____ _____ _____	_____ _____ _____ _____

MyTech Supports

This section is intended for you to develop and save information about your preferred technology.

(You can keep information that helps you to access technology.)

Name

First	Last

Date

MM / DD / YYYY

Email

Website for tech supports (Write down a website that could help you with your connections: ATT.com, iCloud.com, another cell service website, Apple.com, etc.)

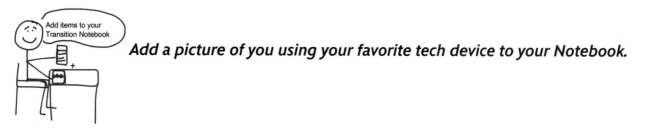

Add a picture of you using your favorite tech device to your Notebook.

Who could help you with technology? (Is there someone you know who is very "techy" and available to help you if you need it? Family, friends, co-worker)

What kind of tech device have you used in the past?

What kind of cell phone do you have?

What are some of your strengths when it comes to using technology.

What are some of your strengths with the following technologies?
- *Cell Phone*
- *Computer*
- *iPad*
- *Tablet*
- *Kindle*

What do you think you could do more easily if you had specific technology?

What do you want to be able to use?

Add items to your Transition Notebook

Add a picture of the device (include price) to your Notebook.

What do you feel helps you the most when using technology?

MyCyberSafety

Use this section to write notes and connect
to ways that you can stay safe online!

● ●

Name

First	Last

Date

	/		/	
MM		DD		YYYY

Email

● ●

Your Online Safety

Here are some questions and ideas about being safe online:

Do you feel safe when using technology? (Technology can involve situations where your safety is taken away. Avoiding dangerous situations is <u>very</u> important. Do you feel safe?)

❑ Yes
❑ No
❑ Most of the time

I would like to find out more about how to make sure I am always safe. (Are you interested in gaining skills and knowledge about staying safe online?)

❑ Yes, that would be great
❑ No, I think I'm good
❑ There are a few questions/concerns that I have

I have had negative experiences online in the past and... (Describe)

Think about how you felt during the time that this happened.

Evaluate the following statements.

	Strongly Disagree	Disagree	Agree	Strongly Agree
I really want to learn more about online safety	❑ 1	❑ 2	❑ 3	❑ 4
I always feel safe online	❑ 1	❑ 2	❑ 3	❑ 4
I always feel unsafe with social media online	❑ 1	❑ 2	❑ 3	❑ 4

I would rate my online safety with these stars:

★ ★ ★ ★ ★ (Circle or highlight your star rating)

. . . .

Here are some "Online Safety" questions for you:

Think carefully about your computer use.

What information should you give out when registering for websites online?

What information would be alright for you to share online?

You receive an email from someone you don't know with the subject line "Hello." What should you do?

What would be a response that would keep you safe?

You are instant messaging with a friend over Skype. Someone you don't know wants to video chat with you. What should you do?

Skype is used for online calling (like a phone) and video chatting. What is your best response to this situation?

You are playing an online game and someone you don't know messages you and says you should "meet up." What should you do?

• Is there something you should say or do?
• Is there someone you should tell about this?

You receive a mean text message on your mobile phone. What should you do?

People can and do say things online or in a text that they would NEVER dare to say to your face. Online stalking/predators and bullying is a serious offense and a crime.
• What would you do in this situation?

You are signing up to participate in an online forum about your favorite TV show. What should you use as a password?

Tell what kind of password—not anything specific or a real password here.
• Should you use your name?
• Should you use identification?
• Should you keep it "generic?"
• Should you use a combination of letters and numbers?

From the options below, which is the safest password? (This should be a creative combination of letters, numbers and symbols. Make sure you find a good way to remember it.)

❑ computer
❑ computer123
❑ CompYouter!7

You are emailing, and in your inbox there is a message that says you've won something. What should you do? (Even though this may sound exciting and fun, this is one way that people try to trick you.)

❑ Open it to see what you've won
❑ Reply to the sender that you don't want those emails
❑ Delete it immediately

Key #4:
"Take a Selfie and Share Your Favorites"

MySelfie and MyFavorites

MySelfie and MyFavorites

This is a form for you to tell about yourself and all of your favorite things. Tell about some of your preferences:

• •

Name

First	Last

Date

	/		/		
MM		DD		YYYY	

• •

Add a SELFIE to your Notebook :) (Use a cell phone, iPad or computer if available. You can print a picture of yourself and add it to your Notebook.)

Who would you most like to spend time hanging out with?

Who do you like to spend extra time with?

What are your favorite FOODS to eat?

What are your favorite things to eat?
- *Breakfast*
- *Lunch*
- *Dinner*
- *Snacks*

What are your favorite MOVIES to watch?

What movies do you like to watch the most?
- *Action*
- *Adventure*
- *Comedy*
- *Drama*

What are your favorite OUTDOOR activities?

What do you like to do outside?
- *Hiking*
- *Boating*
- *Sports*
- *Walks*

What are your favorite SPORTS to watch and/or play?

- *Sports you like to watch on TV or in person*
- *Sports that you like to play*

What are your favorite GAMES to play?

- *Board games*
- *Video games*
- *Group games*

What are your some favorite PLACES you like to go to?

• In your neighborhood
• In your city
• In your state
• In your country
• Internationally

What are your favorite CLOTHES to wear?

When do you feel most comfortable?
• When do you feel most dressed up?
• Is there something that you wear all of the time?

What is your favorite MUSIC to listen to?

Type of music?
• Artist
• Songs

What is your favorite kind of ARTWORK to do or create?

• Painting
• Sculpture
• Photography
• Drawing

MyEvents

Take some time to write down the types of events you have been to and what you would like to attend.

• •

Name

First	Last

Date

MM	/	DD	/	YYYY

• •

 Add a picture of the event you attended to your Notebook.

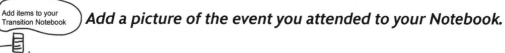

Tell about a really fun event that you have gone to in the past.

When/What/Where have you gone to...
- *A great concert?*
- *A fun sporting event?*
- *A party/wedding?*
- *A family reunion?*
- *An exhibit?*
- *Another celebration?*

Why was the event so much fun for you?

Express yourself:
- *Did you feel great?*
- *Did you connect with people?*
- *Did you love the music?*
- *Did you love what the performance?*
- *Were you surprised by something?*
- *Did you enjoy something new?*

Future goal: A new event in the community that I would like to attend is:

Write a future event goal for yourself: On (Date/Time?) _____, I would like to go to (Event name?)_____ at (Where?)_____ with (Name of person?)_____.

Event #1: Add a document showing the event you would like to attend to your Notebook. (This should be an example: a flier, calendar event or picture of the place/venue.)

Event #1: What are the details of the event?

- *When is it?*
- *Where is it?*
- *Who do you want to go with?*
- *How much will it cost?*
- *How will you get there?*
- *Do you need reservations?*
- *Do you need to purchase anything in advance?*

Event #2: Add a document showing the event you would like to attend to your Notebook. (You could print a .pdf or .jpg showing a flier, calendar event or picture of the place/venue.)

Event #2: What are the details of the event?

- *When is it?*
- *Where is it?*
- *Who do you want to go with?*
- *How much will it cost?*
- *How will you get there?*
- *Do you need reservations?*
- *Do you need to purchase anything in advance?*

MyPlaces

Tell about the places that you really like to go.

● ●

Name

First	Last

Date

MM   DD   YYYY

● ●

My Favorite Places

Write down some of the places you like to go to in your community or on a big adventure.

My favorite places include the following:

❑ Sporting events
❑ Shopping
❑ Being active
❑ Watching fun things
❑ Exploring new things
❑ Adventure
❑ Using my skills physically
❑ Using my skills academically

Add a picture of you at your favorite place to your Notebook.

Add a picture of a favorite place you have been to your Notebook!

Some places in my nearby community that I enjoy are:

Write down some favorite places you like to go to in your community.

My feelings about traveling to new places is:

❑ Very Important

❑ Important

❑ Neutral

❑ Somewhat Important

❑ Not at all Important

❑ Scary

If I were to pick one place to go and didn't have to worry about money or distance, it would be:

This could be somewhere in your city, state, country or international.
- *A place*
- *An event*
- *For fun*
- *For adventure*
- *To try something new*

Why would you want to go to this place?

Have you:
- *Been there before?*
- *Heard people talk about it?*
- *Seen an ad for it?*
- *Been excited to experience things there?*

Some great places in this state where I live are:

If you aren't sure about this one, grab a map and find a place that looks like a fun place to go.

My favorite way to travel is to go by:

❑ Bike

❑ Bus

❑ Car

❑ Train

❑ Airplane

❑ Cruise Ship

Goal: Where would you like to travel to in the next five years?

Write down something like…
By (Date)_____, I would
like to save up ($)_____ and
go to (Where)_____ with
(Who)_____.

Add items to your Transition Notebook

Add a picture of the place you have chosen as your travel goal to your Notebook. (You could attach picture or map of your chosen place.)

MyWeekend Plans *(See Appendix for perforated copy)*

Name

First	Last

Date

| MM | / | DD | / | YYYY |

My favorite part of the week was:

My plan for this weekend is:

Friday Night:

For dinner I would like to have: _____

I will stay up until: _____

Watch a movie: Yes ❏ / No ❏ If so, which one? _____

A friend I could call _____ Their phone # _____

I would like to go to: _____

If I go there, I will: _____

Saturday:

For breakfast I would like to have: _____

For lunch I would like to have: _____

For dinner I would like to have: _____

I will stay up until: _____

Watch a movie: Yes ❑ / No ❑ If so, which one? _____

A friend I could call _____ Their phone # _____

I would like to go to: _____

If I go there, I will: _____

Sunday:

For breakfast I would like to have: _____

For lunch I would like to have: _____

For dinner I would like to have: _____

I will stay up until: _____

Watch a movie: Yes ❑ / No ❑ If so, which one? _____

A friend I could call _____ Their phone # _____

I would like to go to: _____

If I go there, I will: _____

My plan for transportation this weekend:

How are you planning on getting to the things you want to do this weekend?

- *Ask a parent/caregiver?*
- *Carpool with someone?*
- *Share rides to and from?*
- *Take the bus?*
  —*What bus or buses?*
  —*What times?*

How much money will you need for the events you are planning?

- *Will you need to pay to get in?*
- *Will you be ordering something to eat?*
- *Will you need money for the bus?*

Add everything up!

MyTrip Planner *(See Appendix for perforated copy)*

Name

First	Last

Date

MM	DD	YYYY

1. **Where would you like to go in the community?** (Examples are parks, specialty stores, exhibits, exercise facilities, recreational opportunities, etc.)

2. **Why are you interested in going there?**

3. **Who would you want to go with for this trip?**

4. **What are the hours of the places/businesses you would like to go to? Will they be open during the times you want to visit?** (Confirm this by calling or looking up hours online.)

5. **What bus (or buses) do I need to take to get there?**

6. **What time does the bus leave?**

7. **What is my plan for lunch? Am I going to bring lunch from home or buy one in the community?**

8. **What supplies do I need to bring on this outing? How much money do I need?**

MyCommunity

This is a section where you can attach a document of your favorite trip plan for your community.

. . . .

Name

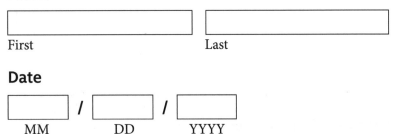

First   Last

Date

| | / | | / | |
MM   DD   YYYY

. . . .

Some of the places I like to go on the public bus:

Write down some of the places that you like to go to on the public bus.

Remember: You can go to your city or county bus system's website to get more information.

Many transit websites have trip planning guides. Use them and attach your trip plans in this section.

Add items to your Transition Notebook

Print copies of your planned trips and add them to your Notebook. (This is where you can add a saved online trip plan so that you can refer back to it later.)

MyBus Trip Plan #1 Location _____

MyBus Trip Plan #2 Location _____

MyBus Trip Plan #3 Location _____

MyBus Trip Plan #4 Location _____

MyBus Trip Plan #5 Location _____

Would you consider riding the public bus by yourself? (Tell about how comfortable you are with riding the public bus by yourself.)

❑ Definitely
❑ Probably
❑ Not Sure
❑ Probably Not
❑ Definitely Not

Tell about your experiences with riding the public bus:

Add some things like…
- *When did you start riding the public bus?*
- *Who helped you to know how to use the bus?*
- *Did you find it difficult? Why?*
- *Has it been positive, negative or both?*

New Routes/New Places:

Write down some of the places that you'd like to visit by bus.

Is there any concern you have about riding the public bus?

- *Does it make you nervous?*
- *What would help you to feel safe?*
- *Who could you talk to about riding the public bus?*
- *Is there someone who could go with you?*

Bus Pass Information:

Tell about the following:
- *Do you currently have a valid bus pass?*
- *Where could you get one in your community?*
- *How can you put money on your card or obtain more tickets?*

There are some tips about how to be safe on the bus online. Some of those ways to be safe are:

Go to your local public bus site online. They will have some information on rider safety.
- *You can also do a general search online.*
- *Make notes of the tips here.*

Add any additional information here:

Add some information about riding public transportation here:
- *Do you have any stories or experiences to share?*
- *Do you need to get or update a bus pass?*
- *Is there someone specific that you would like to have ride the bus with you?*

MyAccess

Write down important information about your access to places in the community.

Very accessible!

• •

Name

First	Last

Date

☐ / ☐ / ☐
MM   DD   YYYY

• •

Personal Information: Accessibility

Write about some details that are important for you to access your community.

Tell about your mobility:

❏ I am able to walk without assistance
❏ I am able to walk with support
❏ I use a manual wheelchair independently
❏ I use a power wheelchair independently
❏ My support provider helps with my mobility

MyMobility: Write about your mobility needs here.

Write some details about your personal mobility.
- What supports do you use?
- How do you care for your own equipment?
- How do you or your support providers care for equipment?

Make a choice: I have _____ **with accessibility.**

- No major problem
- Some concerns and questions
- Significant problem-solving to do
- Full assistance needed

MyMobility: This is where you can make note of some places that have great accessibility:

Which places were very accessible for you?
- Great access to goods/services
- Accommodating staff
- Doors that are easily opened independently
- Wide aisles
- Ramps
- Useful elevators

MyMobility: Where are some places that you have had difficulty accessing?

Write down some accessibility issues they have and how you would change them.

Do you have any mobility goals that you would like to share?

- Some increased independence
- New equipment ideas
- Places you would like to access
- New techniques, tools or skills to learn

Additional Information:

Please take some time to further highlight your individual needs for mobility and getting around as independently as possible.

MyService Ideas

Serving your community is a great thing, both for yourself and others. Write some ideas down about service to others around you.

• •

Name

First	Last

Date

| | / | | / | |
| MM | DD | YYYY |

• •

Ideas for Serving Others

Think of places and people who could use some encouragement or support from you.

My skills that could be helpful for others:

MyMobility: Where are some places that you have had difficulty accessing?

Do you have any mobility goals that you would like to share?

Is there a community group you could help sometime soon?

Community group ideas:
- *YMCA volunteer*
- *Food bank volunteer*
- *Church/Synagogue/Mosque volunteer*
- *Hospital/hospice volunteer*
- *Sports teams*

Are there some friends who could volunteer with you?

Make a list of friends who could volunteer with you.

Make a list of possible volunteer opportunities and events in your community.

Brainstorm with others about places and events for volunteering.
- *Research your community online.*
- *Find times and dates of specific events.*
- *Think about opportunities that you can add to your resume!*

Write the dates of the events as well.

MyFun and Games

This is a section where you are able to tell about the things you like to do for fun, and the games you like to play.

• •

Name

First	Last

Date

[ ] / [ ] / [ ]
MM   DD   YYYY

• •

Add items to your Transition Notebook

Add a picture of yourself playing your favorite game to your Notebook.
(Find a cool picture of yourself having fun and playing your favorite game.)

How important is it for you to play games? (Board games, video games, etc.)
❑ Very Important
❑ Important
❑ Neutral
❑ Somewhat Important
❑ Not at all Important
❑ N/A

Do you prefer to play games where you are active?
❑ Yes
❑ No
❑ No Preference

Do you like to play games as a way to get to know people?
❑ Yes
❑ No
❑ No Preference

Do you like to play games when you stay indoors?
❏ Yes
❏ No
❏ No Preference

Would you like to be so good at a game that you would enter competitions to do it?
❏ Yes
❏ No
❏ No Preference

When you have free-time, what would you prefer to do? (Go ahead and choose one of the following. If you choose "other," write about it below.)

❏ Play video games
❏ Play board games with people
❏ Text or instant message my friends
❏ Put a puzzle together
❏ Go outside and play a sport or game

Write a few sentences telling about your favorite board game.

What is the game?
- *How do you play it?*
- *How many people can play with you?*
- *How long have you played it?*
- *Is it difficult for you or others to learn?*
- *Why do you enjoy it?*

Video Games: What is your favorite game and why?

Tell about the game
- *Who are the characters?*
- *What makes you good at this game?*
- *Who do you play with?*

Is there a game that you are wanting to buy?

This could be any game!
- *How much is it?*
- *Where can you buy it?*
- *Why do you want to get this game?*

Add items to your Transition Notebook

Add a picture of the game you want to buy to your Notebook. (Find a picture on the Internet.)

If you were with a group of people and they wanted you to play a game with them that you didn't know how to play, would you try to learn it and play with them?

❑ Definitely

❑ Probably

❑ Not Sure

❑ Probably Not

❑ Definitely Not

Random Question: If you had to be a cartoon character for a day, who would you be? Why?

- *Pick a character*
- *Why would you want to be that one?*
- *What is this character like?*
- *What adventure would you go on?*
- *What would the end of the day be like for you?*

Additional information or questions:

Is there anything else you would like to add?
- *Specific questions or statements about games that you love?*
- *Something that you would want to put on your birthday or Christmas list?*
- *Are there questions you have about online gaming?*

MySports

Use this section to tell about the sports that you enjoy watching and playing.

Name

First	Last

Date

MM	/	DD	/	YYYY

How important are sports to you in your life? (If sports are not important to you, and you are not interested ...just leave the rest of the form blank.)

 Add items to your Transition Notebook

Add a picture of yourself playing the sport you love to your Notebook. (Find a picture to attach showing yourself enjoying your favorite sport. Also, you can attach a team logo or athlete that you really like.)

Add a picture of your favorite team/logo/athlete.

My favorite sports are:
- ❑ Baseball
- ❑ Football
- ❑ Basketball
- ❑ Soccer
- ❑ Auto Racing
- ❑ Hockey
- ❑ Motorcross
- ❑ Cheerleading
- ❑ Dance
- ❑ Other

Is there another sport that you like, but wasn't listed?

- *Tennis*
- *Lacrosse*
- *Rugby*
- *Other sport*

My favorite NFL (pro) team is: _____

Why do you like this team, and who do you think is the best on the team?

```
┌─────────────────────────────────────────┐
│                                           │
│                                           │
│                                           │
│                                           │
└─────────────────────────────────────────┘
```

My favorite NCAA (college) football team is: _____

Why do you like this team, and who do you think is the best on the team?

```
┌─────────────────────────────────────────┐
│                                           │
│                                           │
│                                           │
│                                           │
└─────────────────────────────────────────┘
```

My favorite NBA (pro basketball) team is: _____

Why do you like this team, and who do you think is the best on the team?

```
┌─────────────────────────────────────────┐
│                                           │
│                                           │
│                                           │
│                                           │
└─────────────────────────────────────────┘
```

My favorite NHL (hockey) team is: _____

Why do you like this team, and who do you think is the best on the team?

```
┌─────────────────────────────────────────┐
│                                           │
│                                           │
│                                           │
│                                           │
└─────────────────────────────────────────┘
```

My favorite NCAA (college) basketball team is: _____

Why do you like this team, and who do you think is the best on the team?

```
┌─────────────────────────────────────────┐
│                                           │
│                                           │
│                                           │
│                                           │
└─────────────────────────────────────────┘
```

Tell about another specific team that you really like to watch:

Do you like to watch...
- *A local baseball team?*
- *A local soccer team?*
- *A local hockey team?*
- *A specific athlete?*

Why do you like this team, and who do you think is the best on the team?

My favorite professional athlete is: _____

Why do you like this specific athlete?

- *Because they are just cool*
- *They have impressive skills doing* _____
- *Your family or friends like them too*

Goal! Write a goal about sports in your life here:

Write a goal for yourself. Here is an example:
By (Date)_____, I would like to try (Write a sports related activity), so that I can enjoy and grow my interest in sports.

MyLibrary

Use this space to share information about your own entertainment media.

• •

Name

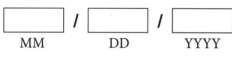

First   Last

Date

[   ] / [   ] / [   ]

MM   DD   YYYY

• •

The things that are the most entertaining for me are: (What are the things you like to have in your library so that you can access them for fun and enjoyment?)

❏ My Music
❏ My Books
❏ My Movies
❏ My Video Games

Make a list of your favorite SONGS/MUSIC:

What type of music do you enjoy?
- *List out your favorite songs and the artist.*

Make a list of your favorite BOOKS to read:

What type of books do you like to read?
- *List out your favorite books to read and the author.*

Make a list of your favorite MOVIES to watch:

What type of movies do you like to watch?
- *List your favorite movie title and actors.*

Make a list of your favorite VIDEO GAMES to play:

What type of video games to play?
- *List your favorite types of video games and the titles.*

Attach a picture or create a drawing of your favorite covers:

- *Music Cover*
- *Book Cover/Titles*
- *Movie Cover/Titles*
- *Video Game Cover*

- *Tell about the reasons why you love each of the items you listed above.*

- *What made you want to get/buy them in the first place.*
- *Who introduced you to these things in your library?*

MyArtwork

This is a great place to tell about your own artwork, and to show off some of your creativity.

•••

Name

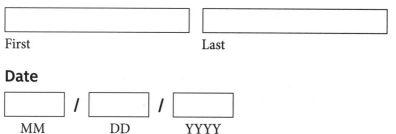

First   Last

Date

[   ] / [   ] / [   ]

MM   DD   YYYY

•••

Describe the type of artwork that you like to create yourself.

- *Do you like to paint?*
- *Do you like to do sculpture?*
- *How about drawing?*
- *Do you like watercolor?*
- *Drawing cartoons characters?*
- *Abstract art?*
- *Art that tells a story?*

Where do you like to create your own artwork?

- *Do you need a lot of space?*
- *Do you like it to be quiet?*
- *Can you do art and other things at the same time?*
- *Do you need access to equipment (like a wheel or kiln)*

What supplies do you need in order to do your artwork?

- *Paints*
- *Brushes*
- *Canvas*
- *Clay*
- *Paper*
- *Cleaning supplies*
- *Tabletop*

MyArt Gallery

Attach some pictures of your best artwork in this section.

Attach a picture to your Notebook: MyArtwork #1 (Describe your artwork here! How and where did you create it?)

Attach a picture: MyArtwork #2 (Add your description below): (Continue to add your artwork and descriptions here. Then attach the pictures after this page or another notebook.)

Attach a picture: MyArtwork #3 (Add your description below):

Attach a picture: MyArtwork #4 (Add your description below):

Attach a picture: MyArtwork #5 (Add your description below):

Attach a picture: MyArtwork #6 (Add your description below):

Attach a picture: MyArtwork #7 (Add your description below):

Have you been to an art gallery or art fair?

- *What did you see there?*
- *What did you like the best?*
- *What did you like the least?*
- *Did you learn something new?*

Research an art gallery online and print the information or the brochure on the next page. (You can also add your flier to this behind this page.)

Take some time to demonstrate some of your great artwork here:

MyStyle

This section will help you to tell about your personal style.
Do you have preferences for your personal style?

....

Name

First	Last

Date

MM		DD		YYYY

....

Add items to your Transition Notebook

Add a picture showing your personal style to your Notebook! (You could attach a picture showing your style with hats, glasses, clothing choices, make-up, and shoes.)

MyStyle Preferences

Let's talk about your personal style and unique look!

What are some of your favorite clothes to wear?

Detail out some of the things that you currently have in your closet and like a lot.

This should be something that makes you feel great!

How would you describe the way you like to dress?

- *Casual/Comfortable*
- *Trendy*
- *Alternative*
- *Sporty*
- *Classic*
- *Business*
- *Formal*

What are some items you would like to add to your personal style?

❏ Hats
❏ Jewelry
❏ Cool shoes
❏ Great jeans
❏ Make-up
❏ Nice dress
❏ Sport jacket/suit and tie
❏ Great handbag/purse
❏ Other _____

List out your five favorite stores for buying clothes/shoes/accessories

Where do you like to find some of your favorite styles?
- *Which mall?*
- *What specific store?*
- *Why do you like that store?*
- *Is it affordable or expensive?*

Write the name of your favorite celebrity and tell why you like their personal style.

If you were to take a look at some of your favorite magazines, what celebrity would you consider having a great "look"

Add items to your Transition Notebook

Add a picture of your favorite celebrity to your Notebook. (Take a picture, and attach your favorite celebrity wearing a "cool look.")

Where do you like to get your fashion and style ideas? (It's fun to see what other people are wearing. Fashion trends come and go, so watching what people are choosing for the latest style can be fun. Where are you looking?)

❏ From friends
❏ From TV
❏ From magazines
❏ From watching people
❏ From online websites

List out some things you would like to add to your wardrobe.

This could be:
- *Pants/jeans*
- *Shirts*
- *Sweatshirts*
- *Accessories*
- *Outerwear*

Additional MyStyle notes:

Are there some specific wardrobe preferences and needs that you have?

Are there some fabrics that you prefer to stay away from?

You can attach one or several pictures of some things you would like to add to your wardrobe to your Notebook.

MyHair Care

Name

First	Last

Date

[ ] / [ ] / [ ]
MM   DD   YYYY

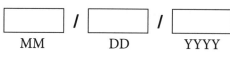

Add items to your Transition Notebook

Add a picture showing your hair preferences to your Notebook. (This picture should be one showing your choice for your personal or favorite hairstyle.)

Do you wash and condition your own hair? (It's very important to keep your hair conditioned so that it stays manageable. Where are you with this?)

❑ Yes, independently
❑ Yes, sometimes I need help though
❑ No, but I would like to try
❑ No, I will always need some assistance

How often do you wash your hair? (Washing your hair regularly keeps it in good condition and keeps it smelling and looking nice. How are you doing with hair washing?)

❑ I wash it every day
❑ I wash it every other day
❑ I wash it a couple of times a week
❑ About once a week

Which of the following hair care products do you use? (Check all that apply) (Hair care products are both fun and necessary for good hair styling. What do you currently use?)

❑ Straightener
❑ Volumizer
❑ Curl activator
❑ Sculpting wax
❑ Conditioner or moisturizer
❑ Heat protector
❑ Other _____

How often do you get your hair cut? (Think about this on average.)

Is there anything about getting your hair cut that you really want to avoid if possible?

- *Are you sensitive to touch?*
- *Does it make you nervous?*
- *Are you sensitive to smells?*
- *Do you have allergies that should be known?*

Is there a specific place you like to go to get your hair cut? Is there a person who you like the best?

Getting your hair cut can be very personal and having the right person cut it can be extremely important.
- *Is there a specific person you prefer to have cut your hair?*

Which of the following hair styling tools do you use at least once a week? (Styling tools are great if they are used right. It is very important to carefully select and use them. What are you able to use right now? Check all that apply.)

❑ Straightening iron
❑ Heated rollers
❑ Crimping iron
❑ Hair dryer
❑ Curling iron
❑ Brush, comb, or pick
❑ Hair trimmer or clippers
❑ Other _____

Which of the following hair styling products do you use at least once a week?
(Check all that apply.)

❑ Natural ingredients
❑ Alcohol-free ingredients
❑ Oil-free ingredients
❑ Petroleum-free ingredients
❑ Dye-free ingredients
❑ Other _____

How willing are you to try a different hair style? (Sometimes, people can get set into their own preferences, but trying something new is a good idea at times. Are you willing to try something new?)

❑ Extremely willing
❑ Very willing
❑ Moderately willing
❑ Slightly willing
❑ Not at all willing

Additionl information about hair care

MyInterest Inventory – MyIntroduction

(Paragraph #1)

My name is _____. I am in the _____ grade at _____. I _____ school because _____. The subject(s) I like best in school is/are _____ _____.

(Paragraph #2)

The book(s) I like to read is/are _____ _____. In the future, I would like to read _____ _____. For sports, I like to play _____ _____. At school, during my free-time, I prefer to _____. The games that I like to play are _____ _____. When I am at home, I _____ _____. The thing I like best about my home is _____ _____. When I watch TV or movies, I like to watch _____ _____ _____. When I listen to music, I like to listen to _____. I do/don't like to sing with the music I listen to.

When I go to a restaurant, I like to eat _____ _____. The restaurants I like are _____ _____, _____, and _____ _____. I get to go out to eat about_____ times per _____. The places I most like to go to are_____ _____, _____ and ___ _____. Some new places I want to explore are _____, _____ and _____.

(Paragraph #3)

The things I like to do with my family or group home are _____
_____, _____, and _____
_____.

Some of the things in life that bother me the most are _____
_____and _____. One of my favorite
people in life is _____. I like
him/her because _____
_____. I think the greatest person is _____
_____ because they are so _____
_____. When I
am done with high school, I want to be known for being _____
_____, _____and _____.

• •

(Paragraph #4) The three things I like to do best in school are _____
_____, _____ and_____
_____. Some of the things I would like to work on
this year are _____
_____
_____
_____.

I would like to learn more about_____.

Key #5:
"Know Yourself Well"

MySelf Assessments

MySelf Assessment

This is an assessment to show how well you are able to evaluate yourself.

. . . .

Name

First   Last

Date

MM   DD   YYYY

. . . .

Emotionally: Here are some things that I feel I am doing really well:

Think about things…
- *At school (classes or assignments)*
- *At work (specific job tasks)*
- *In my relationships*
- *In my home/family (chores?)*
- *My problemsolving abilities*
- *Artwork*
- *Helping others*

Recreationally: Here are some things that I really want to do for fun:

Think about things…
- *Try a new sport*
- *Travel to somewhere new*
- *Learn a new game*
- *Learn a new skill*
- *Go to a sporting event*
- *Theme park? Disneyland*
- *Join a gym*

Educationally: Here are some things that I feel I am doing really well:

Think about things…
- *Am I taking classes that I need to take?*
- *Am I taking classes that are fun for me?*
- *How can I get better grades?*
- *Is there someone who can tutor me with my classes?*

Physically: Here are some things that I feel I am doing really well with my health:

Are you...
- *Working out regularly?*
- *Getting plenty of sleep?*
- *Drinking a lot of water?*
- *Eating well?*

Financially: Here are some ways that I can make more money or manage my money better:

Can you...
- *Do some chores at home?*
- *Get a new or different job?*
- *Sell some things you don't need?*
- *Reduce your payments/bills?*

Do you...
- *Have a written budget?*

Relationally: Here are some things that I do really well in my relationships:

Are you...
- *Spending time with people who build you up and are kind?*
- *Helping/encouraging others?*
- *Writing notes to people?*
- *Calling friends to see how they are?*
- *Texting/emailing nice things to people?*

Spiritually: Here are some things that I do really well to feel connected spiritually:

Are you...
- *Going to church/synagogue/ mosque?*
- *Listening to uplifting music?*
- *Doing yoga?*
- *Meditating/praying?*
- *Talking to someone about spiritual things?*

MyStrengths and Weaknesses

This is where you can document your greatest strengths and weaknesses.

Name

First	Last

Date

[   ] / [   ] / [   ]
MM   DD   YYYY

Do you have a GOOD SENSE OF HUMOR?
❑ Yes
❑ No
❑ Possibly...I need more practice, though.
❑ Not so much!

Do you have a GOOD MEMORY?
❑ Yes
❑ No
❑ Possibly...I need more practice, though.
❑ Not so much!

Do you have a STONG BODY?
❑ Yes
❑ No
❑ Possibly...If I work on getting stronger.
❑ I have some physical limitations.   More Information:_____

Are you a GOOD READER?
❑ Yes
❑ No
❑ With practice I can get better.
❑ I hate reading!

Are you GOOD WITH NUMBERS?

❑ Yes
❑ No
❑ I would like to get better with practice.
❑ I don't really like math or anything with numbers.

Are you a GOOD DECISION-MAKER?

❑ Yes
❑ No
❑ I need to learn how to make choices more quickly.
❑ I prefer to have others make decisions.

Are you good at FOLLOWING A TASK LIST?

❑ Yes
❑ No
❑ I need more practice.
❑ Very difficult for me.   More Information:_____

Do you have GOOD EYE-CONTACT when talking to others?

❑ Yes
❑ No
❑ I need more practice.
❑ This is too difficult for me.

Are you a GOOD LISTENER?

❑ Yes
❑ No
❑ I'm working on it.
❑ This is difficult for me.   More Information:_____

Are you ORGANIZED?

❑ Yes
❑ No
❑ I can be, with a visual model.
❑ I don't really care about staying organized.

Are you FRIENDLY?

❑ Yes
❑ No
❑ I want to make more friends.
❑ I prefer to be by myself.

Are you HELPFUL? (Use the space at right to explain more, if you would like!)
- ❑ Yes
- ❑ No
- ❑ I want to learn how to be more helpful.
- ❑ I have a hard time thinking of ways to help.

Are you ON-TIME AND PUNCTUAL?
- ❑ Yes
- ❑ No
- ❑ I can do well with calendar reminders.
- ❑ I have difficulty with telling time.

Are you good at READING MAPS ?
- ❑ Yes
- ❑ No
- ❑ I can be, with practice.
- ❑ This might be too difficult for me even with practice.

Are you GENTLE AND KIND?
- ❑ Yes
- ❑ Not really
- ❑ At times I can be.
- ❑ This just doesn't come easily for me.

Do you have a lot of ENERGY?
- ❑ Yes
- ❑ Not really
- ❑ At times I can.
- ❑ I typically run low on energy.

Can you STAY FOCUSED for a long period of time?
- ❑ Only for a few hours.
- ❑ Only for about an hour.
- ❑ Only for a few minutes.
- ❑ I have a hard time staying focused.

What are some of your other strengths?

MyStrengths and Weaknesses

Brainstorm Chart

. . . .

My Own Strengths, Weaknesses, and Changes Chart

Strengths	Things to Improve	Changes to Make	Things to Accept

MyStrengths and Work Web

Directions: Write down some of the strengths you listed on your chart and give some examples of your strengths for your future job.

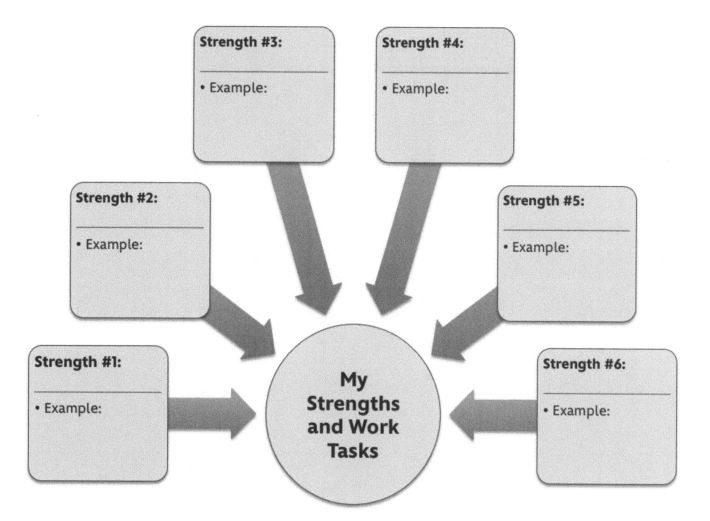

Strength #3:
_____
• Example:

Strength #4:
_____
• Example:

Strength #2:
_____
• Example:

Strength #5:
_____
• Example:

Strength #1:
_____
• Example:

My Strengths and Work Tasks

Strength #6:
_____
• Example:

Now...Let's connect those strengths! Think of some ways to connect those strengths of yours with some tasks where you can use them on the job. In the box below, write down potential vocational tasks that you would perform really well.

Example:

Strength: I am organized.

Task on the job: Stalking shelves, sorting, filing, maintain records

Strength: I am nice and compassionate.

Job Task: Customer service, greeter, answering phone

Write here:

MyStrengths and Weaknesses Write-Up

My name is _____. Some of the strengths that I have are
_____, _____, _____, _____,
and _____. My first strength is that I am _____. I know
that I am because I _____ and I _____
_____. My second strength is that I am
_____. I know that I am because I _____
_____ and I _____.

My third strength is that I am _____. I know that I am because I _____
_____ and I _____
_____. Another strength I have is that I am _____. I know that I
am because I _____ and I _____
_____. Finally, I am also _____. I
know that I am because I _____
and I _____. I know that I will be able to
use these strengths in a job in the future because......

MyStrengths Statement: (Use this box below to make a statement about how your strengths will be
used on the job.)

Key #6:
"Find Careers that Match You"

MyCareer Research

MyCareer

A well-planned career choice involves thinking about the specific work tasks for that job.

∙∙

Name

First	Last

Date

[   ] / [   ] / [   ]
MM   DD   YYYY

∙∙

MyStrengths

Describe how your skills and abilities (from your "MyStrengths" brainstorm chart) relate to the specific tasks for your chosen job.

Strength #1   Work Task

Strength #2   Work Task

Strength #3   Work Task

Strength #4   Work Task

Strength #5

Work Task

Strength #6

Work Task

· ·

MyJob Choice

Directions: First, write the title of the job you would like to have in the future and add your name. Next, write down the tasks that you might be asked to do on the job. Those potential tasks should align as much as possible to your personal strengths that you have written about yourself.

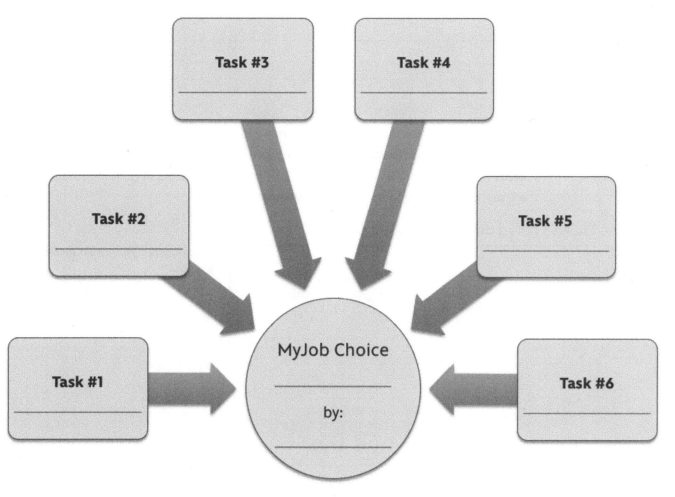

MyCareer Research

This will help you take a closer look at the job choice you are considering for your future.

Name

|_____| |_____|
First   Last

Date

|_____| / |_____| / |_____|
MM   DD   YYYY

MyJob Choice: What job would you like to do in the future?

| |
| |
| |
| |
| |
| |
| |

Write the TITLE of the job choice you are wanting to make.

 Add items to your Transition Notebook

Website: You can use the internet to get more information about your choice. Ask a career counselor for some great websites to gain information. You can search online sources to find information about specific jobs or career clusters to gain information. Then, use the information for the questions that follow.

Specific TASKS I could do on the job are:

| |
| |
| |
| |
| |
| |

Explain what you would do on the job.

The KNOWLEDGE I would need to have:

Explain the specific knowledge you would need for this job.

The EXPERIENCE I would need to have:

Is there any previous training or experience you would need to have before doing this type of job?

Specific SKILLS I would need to have are:

Explain the skills you would need for this job.

The right PERSONALITY for this job are:

List the personality and strengths you would need for this job.

The ABILITIES I would need to have are:

What are some of the physical abilities you would need to be successful?

The TECHNOLOGY I would need to know how to use would be:

List some examples of the technology used.

The EDUCATION I would need to have for this job would be:

What training or certification would you need?

The JOB OUTLOOK for this career choice is:

Write down the future outlook and the salary (money) you could make on average.
- *What about for your state?*
- *Locally?*

Is there anything more you would like to add to your career research?

- *Something we didn't touch on here.*
- *Natural supports provided in this type of work.*
- *Changes that may be coming in the future.*

MyCareer Research Report Outline

Name: _____

Chosen JOB TITLE: _____

- Introduction sentence: I am most interested in _____ because
  _____
  _____
  _____

- Supporting Sentence 1: Some core tasks include ...
  _____
  _____
  _____

- Supporting Sentence 2: If I were a _____ I would work in
  a place that is...
  _____
  _____
  _____

- Supporting Sentence 3: **Most people would work** (How many hours and/or days?)
  _____
  _____
  _____

- Supporting Sentence 4: Add one more thing you have learned about the workplace.
  _____
  _____
  _____

- Supporting Sentence 5: **The typical earnings are...**
  _____
  _____
  _____

- **Supporting Sentence 6: The education and training I will need include** (2-year degree, 4-year degree, additional classes or additional training...)

  _____

  _____

  _____

- **Supporting Sentence 7: I will need to be able to....**

  _____

  _____

  _____

- **Supporting Sentence 8: I will need to learn how to...**

  _____

  _____

  _____

- **Conclusion Sentence:** (You write this on your own.)

  _____

  _____

  _____

MyCareer Research Write-Up

Use the space below to write out your rough draft of your "MyCareer Research Report." You can then type your final copy and add it to your Transition Notebook.

MyResume – Resume Development

This information will help you start your resume!

Name

First	Last

My Home Address

Street Address

City	State / Province / Region

Postal / Zip Code

My Email Address

My Phone Number

###	###	####

My Education History

List the schools you attended and the dates you were there.

My Elementary School Name

Elementary School Address

Street Address

City	State / Province / Region

Postal / Zip Code

Date Attended – Start:

[____] / [____] / [____]
  MM   DD   YYYY

Finish:

[____] / [____] / [____]
  MM   DD   YYYY

Middle School/Junior High School Name

[_____]

Middle School/Junior High School Address

[_____]

Street Address

[_____]   [_____]

City   State / Province / Region

[_____]

Postal / Zip Code

Date Attended – Start:

[____] / [____] / [____]
  MM   DD   YYYY

Finish:

[____] / [____] / [____]
  MM   DD   YYYY

High School Name

[_____]

High School Address

[_____]

Street Address

[_____]   [_____]

City   State / Province / Region

[_____]

Postal / Zip Code

Date Attended – Start:

[____] / [____] / [____]
  MM   DD   YYYY

Finish:

[____] / [____] / [____]
  MM   DD   YYYY

• •

My References

Think of some people who could be contacted about your work performance. (No family members)

Personal Reference #1

First	Last

Relationship/Position   **Years Known**

Phone Number

[ ] – [ ] – [ ]
####

Personal Reference #2

First	Last

Relationship/Position   **Years Known**

Phone Number

[ ] – [ ] – [ ]
####

Personal Reference #3

First	Last

Relationship/Position   **Years Known**

Phone Number

[ ] – [ ] – [ ]
####

Work History

List some places you have worked and the dates you were there.

Work Location/Position Title #1

[   ]

[   ]
Street Address

[   ]   [   ]
City   State / Province / Region

[   ]
Postal / Zip Code

From:

[   ] / [   ] / [   ]
 MM   DD   YYYY

To:

[   ] / [   ] / [   ]
 MM   DD   YYYY

Work Location/Position Title #2

[   ]

[   ]
Street Address

[   ]   [   ]
City   State / Province / Region

[   ]
Postal / Zip Code

From:

[   ] / [   ] / [   ]
 MM   DD   YYYY

To:

[   ] / [   ] / [   ]
 MM   DD   YYYY

Work Location/Position Title #3

Street Address

City   State / Province / Region

Postal / Zip Code

From:

[ ] / [ ] / [ ]
MM   DD   YYYY

To:

[ ] / [ ] / [ ]
MM   DD   YYYY

MyEmployment Application-Practice

Fill this out to practice writing the information needed
to get a job of your choice!

• •

Your Contact Information

Name

First	Last

Date

_____ / _____ / _____
 MM   DD   YYYY

Address

_____
Street Address

City	State / Province / Region

_____
Postal / Zip Code

My Email Address

_____

My Phone Number

_____ – _____ – _____
 ###   ###   ####

Social Security Number (Please keep this information confidential. If you are not ready to input this and keep it secure, just write "N/A" for now.)

_____

Which position are you applying for? (Restaurant/Food Service Worker? Pet Care Attendant/Pet Store Worker? Sporting Goods Retail Store Worker? Video Game Retail Staff? Assistive Living/Care Attendant? Bookstore/Library Assistant? Office Assistant? Event Staff? Retail Store - Stock Clerk? Other?)

[   ]

Are you employed now?
❏ Yes
❏ No

If so, may we inquire of you present workplace? (Is it okay with you that this employer contacts your current supervisor, or from a job you had in the past?)
❏ Yes
❏ No

When can you start?

[   ] / [   ] / [   ]
MM   DD   YYYY

ePortfolio Web Site (If you do not have an online portfolio, just place "N/A" in the box.)

[http://   ]

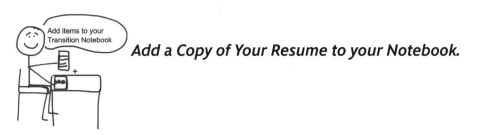 *Add a Copy of Your Resume to your Notebook.*

Desired Income: Hourly rate (How much would you like to make per hour? **Make sure this is consistent with average wages in the community where you live and work.**)

$ [   ] . [   ]
Dollars   Cents

Subjects of Special Study or Research Work

[   ]

Special Skills

[   ]

Activities

[   ]

U.S. Military or Naval Service

[ ]

List Education History

[ ]

- *School/dates attended*
- *Diploma or certificate?*

List References

[ ]

- *Name of family/friend*
- *Volunteering?*
- *Name of company*
- *Dates of employment*

MyInterview Practice

This will help you with common interview questions and prepare for a real interview.

• •

Name

First	Last

Date

	/		/	
MM	DD	YYYY

• •

Common Interview

Think of some good answers to these questions. Remember to use complete sentences.

Tell me about yourself. What would you like to share?

Think about telling the interviewer about some of the following things:
- *Where you are from?*
- *State some highlights of your education and work history.*

What brings you to this company, and why are you interested in this position?

You can answer with something like: "First, I would like to get experience _____. Then, gain the knowledge to _____. Lastly, I would love to _____.

I can help your company _____."

What is your availability for the position? Are you willing to work more than part-time?

Make sure to give an honest answer as to how long you could work in this particular job per week.

What are some skills you have that would pertain to this job?

Think about an answer like the following:
"My skills that would pertain to working as a _____ are: First, _____, next I love _____. Lastly, I work well _____."

Tell about your experiences. Have you done similar work before?

Reflect on your past experiences working in a similar job. Make some comments about how those experiences will help you.

Tell about your teamwork. Do you usually get along well with other people/co-workers?

I usually like to:
- *Work alone*
- *Work with just one other*
- *Work in a group*

Give some examples of how you work well in a team or by yourself.

How long have you been interested in this type of job?

When did you first know that you wanted to do this type of work?
- *Do you know someone who does similar work?*
- *What is the most interesting thing about it?*

Describe what you do to prepare for an interview. Then, follow this to do some mock interview experiences with peers or adults.

How do you think you did when practicing for your interview?
- *Did you feel confident?*
- *Did you give answers quickly?*
- *Did you stay focused and positive?*
- *Were you able to ask your own questions?*
- *Did you feel comfortable with the interviewer?*
- *Is there anything you would do differently next time?*

Remember... practice makes perfect so be sure to practice often!

Key #7: "Know Where You're Going"

MyTransition Plans

MyTransition Plans

Use this section to attach your transition plan.

••

Name

First	Last

Date

[ ] / [ ] / [ ]
MM   DD   YYYY

••

My Most Recent Transition Plan

Your IEP case manager needs to write your transition plan for your IEP team. What would you like for people to know about your plans for the future?

My Current Transition Plan (Add a copy of your current transition plan to your Notebook. This should be connected to your IEP or Independent Living Plan.)

••

MyTransition Plan Goals

Let's work on developing some goals that you might have for yourself!

What are some things that you would like to include in your transition planning? (Pick out some things that you would like to focus on here.)

❑ A job of my choice
❑ Drive a car
❑ Have an apartment
❑ Go to a community college
❑ Get into a recreation club
❑ Play a sport
❑ Travel to another state/country
❑ Learn a new skill or sport
❑ Perform on stage
❑ Learn some cooking skills
❑ Other _____

Tell about the things you selected:

What is it about those things that seem exciting or fun for you?

Write a vocational (work) goal for yourself in the box below:

By (date)_____, I would like to be able to work at (place/location)_____ and be able to(what?)_____(for how long?)_____.

Write a home/living goal for yourself here:

By (date)_____, I would like to be able to live at (place/location)_____ and be able to(what?)_____(for how long?)_____.

Write a recreational goal for yourself—think of some fun things to do!

By (date)_____, I would like to be able to have fun at (place/location)_____ and be able to(what?)_____(for how long?)_____.

Write your educational/training goal for yourself in this section:

By (date)_____, I would like to be able to (learn what?)_____ (where?) _____ (how often/ duration/how well?)_____.

Example: *By next year, I would like to be able to learn to do sculpture at _____ College, attending class 1x per week for one semester.*

How do you feel about your future plans?

Do you feel:
- *Excited?*
- *Nervous?*
- *Happy?*
- *Hopeful?*
- *A sense of freedom?*

Who are the people who have helped you the most with your transition plan?

This is a section where you can tell about the people who have helped you develop your goals for the future.
- *Who are they?*
- *What did they help you with?*
- *Why are they helpful?*
- *Why are these people important to you?*

Additional Comments:

Your transition plan is one of the most important life planning documents!

Is there anything else that you would like to add to this section?

MyTransition Pictures – Scavenger Hunt

Follow the steps below to create a visual display of your transition plans

Name

First	Last

Date

	/		/	
MM		DD		YYYY

❑ Open up a word processing document (i.e., Word, Notability, etc.)

❑ Create a new file and create the title, "MyTransition Pictures Scavenger Hunt."

❑ Find and add pictures of the following transition areas in a Google search:

   ❑ A house or apartment you would love to live in

   ❑ A pet you would like to have

   ❑ A job that you would want

   ❑ A place you would like to travel to

   ❑ Transportation—The way you will get to work (Bus/Car)

   ❑ Clothes that you would like to wear

   ❑ A cell phone you would like to have

   ❑ A sport you would like to try

   ❑ A store that you would like to do your shopping

   ❑ Something you want to do in your free time

MyTransition Plan - Simplified Outline

Something new is coming my way!

Name

First	Last

Date

[   ] / [   ] / [   ]
MM   DD   YYYY

1. MyWork:

I would like to work at _____.

I want to work there because _____.

2. My Fun: Right now for fun, I...

Want to learn how to _____.

Would like to spend time with _____.

3. My Home: Right now, I live with _____.

In the future, I would like to live in _____.

I would like to live with _____.

4. My Transportation:

Right now, I get around by _____.

In the future, I would like to get to work and other activities by _____.

MyTransition Plan Essay: (Use the information from above for a brief essay.)

[   ]

Key #8:
"Lead Your Own IEP"

MyIEP and Transcripts

MyIEP

This is a place to think about and document your most recent IEP. This will help share your school experiences and the supports that you need.

Name

First   Last

Date

	/		/	

MM   DD   YYYY

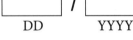 **Add a copy of your IEP to your Notebook.**

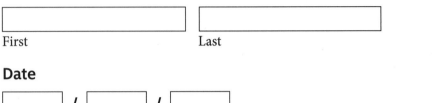

MyAcademics Goal #1

1. What area is this goal in?
   - Reading
   - Writing
   - Math
   - Organization
2. Write out the goal.

MyAcademics Goal #2

1. What area is this goal in?
   - Reading
   - Writing
   - Math
   - Organization
2. Write out the goal.

MyAcademics Goal #3

> 1. What area is this goal in?
>   - Reading
>   - Writing
>   - Math
>   - Organization
> 2. Write out the goal.

MySocial Skills Goal #1

> 1. What specific skill are you working on with peers and/or adults?
> 2. Write out the goal.

MySocial Skills Goal #2

> 1. What specific skill are you working on with peers and/or adults?
> 2. Write out the goal.

How do you feel about the goals that you are working on?

> Do you feel like...
>   - You will be able to reach your goals?
>   - Changing any goals?
>   - You would like to add any goals?

What helps you the most when you are learning new things?

When working on your personal goals, do you like...

- *Someone to guide you along?*
- *To try things on your own?*
- *Having a schedule to help you know start and finish points?*

How do you feel about telling others about your IEP?

Would you want to...

- *Lead your own meeting to discuss it?*
- *Have others talk about it with you?*
- *Have an audio version of your IEP?*

What are one or two goals you would like to work on?

This could be any academic, social, vocational or related service goal that you would like to pursue.

What are some accommodations you can get in class or on state testing because of your IEP?

Can you ask your teacher for...

- *Additional time on tests or assignments?*
- *A change in seating?*
- *A change in setting for tests?*
- *A scribe?*
- *The directions to be read aloud?*
- *Shortened assignments?*
- *Others?*

Add items to your Transition Notebook

Add a copy of your "Student-Led IEP Meeting" PowerPoint slides to your Notebook. (Use My Key's MyStudent-Led IEP forms to document your preferences. It is a guided format for your use in IEP meetings. Add any additional information that you would like to include in your Individualized Education Plan. These can be found at mykeyplans.com)

MyStudent – Led IEP Meeting

(*See Appendix for perforated copy*)

This activity will help you to pan for your IEP meeting. You can use this to help guide you in leading a portion of your own meeting... It's all about YOU!

Name

First	Last

Date

| MM | / | DD | / | YYYY |

Introduction

Who is at your meeting?

- **You:**
- **Case Manager:**
- **District Representative:**
- **Parent/Guardian:**
- **DVR Counselor:**
- **Employment Vendor:**

Purpose of the Meeting

We are meeting today to go over my progress on goals, my transition plan, and my future goals.

My current goals are:

The accommodation that I get in my classes for assignments and tests are:

Vision for the Future

What do you want for your life in these areas:

- Career:
- Family:
- Housing:
- Transportation:
- Fun/Friends/ Recreation:

....

Goals

How have you done on your goals with your current IEP?

What are the goals that you would like to be working on this next year?

Learning Style

My learning style is important for others to know. When an idea or work is presented to me, I have found that it is best if people know more about my style.

My best learning style is...

❏ Visual Learner: Watching

❏ Kinesthetic: Feeling/Doing

❏ Auditory: Listening

❏ Multi-Sensory: Several modes

I learn new skills best when people:

❏ Show me what to do.

❏ Let me work with my hands, feel it and try it.

❏ Just tell me how to do something and let me try.

❏ Use different ways: Show me, let me try it, and tell me as well.

My Portfolio

Here is my current portfolio

In it, you will see:

- 1.
- 2.
- 3.
- 4.
- 5.

My Case Manager:

My IEP is written, updated and reported on by:

[   ]

- I would now like for my case manager to talk about some of the details of my plan.

- We will show the team a copy of my IEP.

- Thank you for being here!

Additional information/notes from MyIEP Meeting:

[ ]

MyTranscripts

This is the section where you can document and add copies of your transcripts from the schools you attended.

• •

Name

First   Last

Date

[MM] / [DD] / [YYYY]

• •

School #1 (Most Recent School):

What grades? Dates? This could be a middle school, high school/transition or college/technical school.

Add a copy of your transcript to your Notebook. (The registrar, counselor or teacher should be able to assist you in getting a copy of your transcript.)

• •

School #2

What grades? Dates? If there is no other school, just type "n/a" in the school name field.

Add a copy of this school transcript to your Notebook.

• •

School #3

What grades? Dates? If there is no other school, just type "n/a" in the school name field.

Add a copy of this school transcript to your Notebook.

• •

Any additional information to share about school experiences?

Is there any educational history that you would like to explain further?

Make some additional comments here!

Key #9:
"Create A Great Project to Show Your Work"

MyCulminating Project

MyCulminating Project: MyVisual Portfolio

Directions for Creating a Great Project

. . . .

1. When you have completed the *My Transition Portfolio* to this point...do the following:

❑ Organize all of your work into proper sections in your Notebook.

❑ On a computer or other device, find images that reflect the information you have gathered in each section.

❑ Collect and label all images, highlighting your preferences.

❑ Save images into a folder with your name on it. You will use these in iMovie or another application to create your project. Save them to a flash drive, Google Drive, etc.

2. Go to a desktop or laptop

❑ Create a new folder for your new project on your computer.

❑ Download your images to new folder.

❑ Import images into iPhoto or other picture application

❑ Make any necessary edits

❑ Be sure to save all of your work

❑ Review your picture collection with teacher or supervisor

3. Open "iMovie"

❑ Drag images onto "iMovie" pane

❑ Create a new movie

4. Creating a movie

❑ Pick a movie theme

❑ Drag pictures into the "movie edit section"

❑ "Command" "click" on all the pictures and drag them into the bottom library field *(they might not go all at the same time but keep going a few at a time)*

❑ Select a Title Slide: "MyVisual Portfolio" By: *(add Your Name)*

❑ Select/replace the transitions between each slide. Adjust as needed.

❑ Select any music to play over your project

❑ Use the voice-over features to talk about your ideas and preferences

❑ Add a slide at the end to show credits

**For a full iMovie tutorial, please refer to iMovie application help, or YouTube a tutorial.

iMovie Project: MyScript

Video Project: MyPortfolio Contents

Use an iPad or Video Camera to Record...Have fun, and use your great personality! (This is an EXAMPLE. Please design your own script based on your own great project.)

Say:

- "This is my living/vocational portfolio • I will talk about the content of my portfolio.

- First, I have MyDream. It tells about the dreams I have for life after high school.

- Next, I have MyStory. It tells about the story of my life – Past, Present and Future.

- After that, I have information about MySpeech and MyCommunication Skills. It tells about how I communicate with others.

- Then, I have MySelf Assessment, which tells about how I feel I am doing in several areas of life.

- I also have a section about MyStrengths and Weaknesses. I show them through brainstorming webs and an essay.

- Then, I have MySelfie and MyFavorites where I have pictures of myself, and my favorite things.

- Next, I have MyInterest Inventory. I wrote an essay about my interests in life.

- I also added some information about MySchedule. This tells about my daily schedule.

- MyResume section is next. I planned what I would write and have a completed resume. I also have a Pocket Resume to take with me to apply for a job.

- Lastly, I have some practice applications that I have filled out.

- Thank you for reviewing MyPortfolio with me!"

Key #10: "Celebrate and Move On"

MyGraduation and Adult Life

MyTransition and Adult Life

Share some information about what your transition out of high school into adult life was/is like:

• •

Name

First   Last

Date

MM   /   DD   /   YYYY

• •

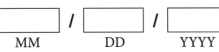

Add a picture of yourself at graduation or as an adult showing yourself in life after your school years to your Notebook.

What was it like for you to go through graduation?

• How did you feel? Nervous, excited, hopeful?
• What was it like to walk across the stage?
• Did you feel like you would miss being in high school?

Post-Secondary Education/Training

After high school, did you go to a school or training program?

Did you complete an entire term (quarter/semester) in the college or training program setting?

What was it like...
- *Difficult?*
- *Easy?*
- *Fun?*
- *Exciting?*

Have you connected with Vocational Rehabilitation?

- *Do you have a counselor?*
- *Have you created a plan for work?*
- *Do you have a job coach or job developer?*
- *Do you need to get connected with someone to see if you qualify for services?*

Have you worked 90 days or more on the job?

❑ Yes
❑ No
❑ Not applicable

Were you paid at least minimum wage on the job?

❑ Yes
❑ No
❑ Not applicable

Describe your job

- *What are the various tasks that you do?*
- *What is your schedule like?*
- *What does your boss expect you to keep doing or do differently?*
- *Is anything really difficult about your job?*

How does it feel for you to be an adult?

*   *What is good about it?*
*   *What is challenging about adulthood?*
*   *Do you feel you have more freedom?*

What are some of your adult responsibilities that you didn't have when you were in school?

*   *Do you have different expectations from family?*
*   *Do you have different schedules to follow?*
*   *Do you feel like your body is changing in some way?*

Are there some adult community groups that you would like to belong to?

Would you like to be in...
*   *An art club?*
*   *A sports club?*
*   *A social skills group?*
*   *A technology group?*

In the future, would you like to have your own family?

Do you want...
*   *To get married?*
*   *To have kids?*
*   *To stay single?*

Where do you like to shop?

Do you have your own money now to spend? What are the stores you like to go to for...
*   *Grocery shopping*
*   *Clothes shopping*
*   *Mall shopping*

Additional Information:

Is there anything else you would like to add about your life experiences now that you are an adult and gaining more independence?

Key #11:
"Get Acquainted With Work"

MyWork Information

MyCo-Workers

This is a section where you could share information about the co-workers you have or had in the past.

● ●

Name

First	Last

Date

MM	DD	YYYY

● ●

MyCo-Workers

Go ahead and write down some information about your current or past co-workers

List your co-workers' names and a little about them here.

- *First and last names*
- *What do they do at work?*
- *How do you know them?*

Who do you feel like you connect with best at work?

Is there someone who has been very helpful, kind, or you have something in common with?

If you had a problem at work, who could you ask for help?

If you were unsure of what to do, who could you ask for help?

What are some "conversation starters" you could use at work?

[blank box]

- *How are you today?*
- *How was your weekend?*
- *How has your family been?*
- *Compliment them on something related to work.*

Call-In Contacts

[blank box]

If you had to call-in sick or ask for someone to take your shift, who could you call?
- *A supervisor*
- *Someone who you work closely with*

Contact #1

[blank box] [blank box]

First   Last

Phone Number

[blank box] – [blank box] – [blank box]

\#\#\#   \#\#\#   \#\#\#\#

Think about this:
When you call-in sick, what information should you give to people at work?

- *Greeting*
- *State your name*
- *Ask for the person in charge*
- *Tell them why you are calling in*
- *Ask for an adjustment in your schedule*
- *Thank them!*

Contact #2

[blank box] [blank box]

First   Last

Phone Number

[blank box] – [blank box] – [blank box]

\#\#\#   \#\#\#   \#\#\#\#

MyScripts: Calling In Sick

[blank box]

Practice and consider the following example: "Hi, this is (your name)_____. I need to let (supervisor's name) _____ know that I will not be able to come in to work. I will return to work on (return date)_____."
Go ahead and create your own script here.

MyWork Conversations

Here are some things that you can use to start conversations with your co-workers or customers (if appropriate).

. . . .

Name

First	Last

Date

	/		/	
MM		DD		YYYY

. . . .

Where do you work? _____

How could you introduce yourself?

Make sure that you look someone in the eye when you introduce yourself!

Be the first to ask your co-worker about their family. What can you say?

Sometimes people don't like to share personal information about their family. Be careful with this one. It could be too personal for some people.

Do you live with your family?

ON MONDAYS...What could you ask about someone's weekend?

This is something that should only be asked if you have a strong connection with someone.
Follow-up questions:
- *Did you have a nice weekend?*
- *What did you do for fun?*
- *Did you go away?*

What could you ask about the weather?

This is something that can be asked of anyone, since it is not too personal and is a very common question.

What could you ask about your co-worker's pets?

This is a very common topic of conversation too. You could ask about:
- *Pet's names*
- *Breed*
- *Tricks that they know*
- *How long they have had their pet*

What questions could you ask about your co-worker's schedule?

- *How long are you working today?*

Again...be careful with this question. It could be considered "too personal."

What can you ask your co-worker about their entertainment and fun?

Does your coworker...
- *Go to sporting events?*
- *Go to movies?*
- *Go to exhibits?*
- *Travel?*
- *Watch the kind of sports you like?*

Appropriateness in conversations while working:

- *When is the best time to have conversations with coworkers?*
- *What are some things to approach a boss or supervisor with in conversation?*
- *What are some ways that you can be reminded to...*
  —Stay on task
  —Stay on topic
  —Use jokes appropriately

MyWork Assessments

This is a place for you to attach the assessments
that you have done with school or vocational rehabilitation.

Name

First	Last

Date

MM	DD	YYYY

What are some areas of strength for you at work?

*List out some of the good things
you are able to do at work. Be
specific about how you see these as
strengths.*

Add a document, or documents, to your Notebook. (These could be work
assessments that a teacher or counselor did with you in high school.)

Add a document to your Notebook: "MyVocational Assessment #1"

Workplace Name/Date:

Add a document to your Notebook: "MyVocational Assessment #2"

Workplace Name/Date:

Add a document to your Notebook: "MyVocational Assessment #3"

Workplace Name/Date:

Add a document to your Notebook: "MyVocational Assessment #4" (These could be assessments that vocational counselors did with you in your post-school years.)

Workplace Name/Date:

Add a document to your Notebook: "MyVocational Assessment #5"

Workplace Name/Date:

Add a document to your Notebook: "MyVocational Assessment #6"

Workplace Name/Date:

Additional Information and Personal Reflection on Work Assessments:

(Did you agree? Or, do you feel differently about your work performance?)

MyVocational Evaluation (Example) *(See Appendix for perforated copy)*

....

Worksite: _____

Job: _____

Name: _____

Month: _____

Job Coach: _____

General

1. Puts personal belongings away in proper place	Yes ❑	No ❑	Emerging Skill ❑	N/A ❑
2. Greets co-workers/friendly	Yes ❑	No ❑	Emerging Skill ❑	N/A ❑
3. Checks in, gets assignment	Yes ❑	No ❑	Emerging Skill ❑	N/A ❑
4. Friendly to members	Yes ❑	No ❑	Emerging Skill ❑	N/A ❑
5. Completes weekly time sheets	Yes ❑	No ❑	Emerging Skill ❑	N/A ❑

Cleaning

6. Uses & changes cleaning cloths, as instructed	Yes ❑	No ❑	Emerging Skill ❑	N/A ❑
7. Uses proper cleaner for glass, pink cleaner for other surfaces	Yes ❑	No ❑	Emerging Skill ❑	N/A ❑
8. Applies spray to surfaces or cloths, as instructed	Yes ❑	No ❑	Emerging Skill ❑	N/A ❑
9. Wipes tables systematically	Yes ❑	No ❑	Emerging Skill ❑	N/A ❑
10. Straightens chairs	Yes ❑	No ❑	Emerging Skill ❑	N/A ❑
11. Tidies objects in the work environment	Yes ❑	No ❑	Emerging Skill ❑	N/A ❑
12. Wipes window sills	Yes ❑	No ❑	Emerging Skill ❑	N/A ❑
13. Sanitizes door handles throughout facility	Yes ❑	No ❑	Emerging Skill ❑	N/A ❑
14. Sanitizes all railings	Yes ❑	No ❑	Emerging Skill ❑	N/A ❑
15. Sanitizes drinking fountain handles and buttons	Yes ❑	No ❑	Emerging Skill ❑	N/A ❑

Cleans windows & other glass, inside & out, streak free

16. Lobby	Yes ❑	No ❑	Emerging Skill ❑	N/A ❑
17. Front door	Yes ❑	No ❑	Emerging Skill ❑	N/A ❑
18. Other entrance door	Yes ❑	No ❑	Emerging Skill ❑	N/A ❑
19. Sanitizes door handles throughout facility	Yes ❑	No ❑	Emerging Skill ❑	N/A ❑
20. Sanitizes stairway railing	Yes ❑	No ❑	Emerging Skill ❑	N/A ❑

Wipes down equipment

21. Works from bottom to top	Yes ❑	No ❑	Emerging Skill ❑	N/A ❑
22. Works systematically	Yes ❑	No ❑	Emerging Skill ❑	N/A ❑
23. Cleans equipment thoroughly	Yes ❑	No ❑	Emerging Skill ❑	N/A ❑
24. Selects equipment to be cleaned next, as instructed	Yes ❑	No ❑	Emerging Skill ❑	N/A ❑

Conduct

25. General conduct acceptable to this workplace	Yes ❑	No ❑	Emerging Skill ❑	N/A ❑
26. Absent rate below 9%	Yes ❑	No ❑	Emerging Skill ❑	N/A ❑
27. Grooming & hygiene	Yes ❑	No ❑	Emerging Skill ❑	N/A ❑
28. Clothing appropriate to this worksite	Yes ❑	No ❑	Emerging Skill ❑	N/A ❑

Communication & Problem Solving

29. Shows good work ethic, energy & enthusiasm	Yes ❑	No ❑	Emerging Skill ❑	N/A ❑
30. Customer service (or task completion) knowledge, manners	Yes ❑	No ❑	Emerging Skill ❑	N/A ❑
31. Polite & friendly to staff (knows names)	Yes ❑	No ❑	Emerging Skill ❑	N/A ❑
32. Requests accommodations as needed	Yes ❑	No ❑	Emerging Skill ❑	N/A ❑
33. Remembers instructions & details	Yes ❑	No ❑	Emerging Skill ❑	N/A ❑
34. Follows chain of command for questions, general info, etc.	Yes ❑	No ❑	Emerging Skill ❑	N/A ❑
35. Knows location of equipment & supplies	Yes ❑	No ❑	Emerging Skill ❑	N/A ❑
36. Knows layout of worksite	Yes ❑	No ❑	Emerging Skill ❑	N/A ❑
37. Adjusts own work-speed for specific task & workload	Yes ❑	No ❑	Emerging Skill ❑	N/A ❑
38. Sets up an efficient workspace	Yes ❑	No ❑	Emerging Skill ❑	N/A ❑
39. Evaluates & adjusts for quality of own work	Yes ❑	No ❑	Emerging Skill ❑	N/A ❑

Safety

40. Uses proper equipment & supplies for the task	Yes ❑	No ❑	Emerging Skill ❑	N/A ❑
41. Returns equipment & supplies to proper place	Yes ❑	No ❑	Emerging Skill ❑	N/A ❑
42. Handles spills safely & as instructed	Yes ❑	No ❑	Emerging Skill ❑	N/A ❑
43. Uses sharp tools safely & as instructed	Yes ❑	No ❑	Emerging Skill ❑	N/A ❑
44. Uses cleaners or chemicals safely & as instructed	Yes ❑	No ❑	Emerging Skill ❑	N/A ❑
45. Lifts safely & as instructed	Yes ❑	No ❑	Emerging Skill ❑	N/A ❑
46. Recognizes potential hazards	Yes ❑	No ❑	Emerging Skill ❑	N/A ❑

Key #12:
"Connect with Supportive Agencies"

MyAdult Service Agencies

MyAgencies

In this section, you can keep a record of agency providers you work with currently or in the future.

....

Name

First	Last

Date

/	/
MM	DD	YYYY

....

Case Manager, State DDA

Keep a record of this agency with their contact info and update it as necessary.

Name

First	Last

Address

Street Address

City	State / Province / Region

Postal / Zip Code

Email Address

Phone Number

–	–
###	###	####

Add a flier or agency brochure to your Notebook.

....

Housing Specialist

Keep a record of this agency with their contact info and update it as necessary.

Name

First	Last

Address

Street Address

City	State / Province / Region

Postal / Zip Code

Email Address

Phone Number

[ ] – [ ] – [ ]
####

Add items to your Transition Notebook

Add a flier or agency brochure to your Notebook.

• •

Vocational Rehabilitation/Work

Keep a record of this agency with their contact info and update it as necessary.

Name

First	Last

Address

Street Address

City	State / Province / Region

Postal / Zip Code

Email Address

[ ]

Phone Number

[ ] – [ ] – [ ]
####

Add items to your Transition Notebook

Add a flier or agency brochure to your Notebook.

. . . .

Employment Agency Vendor

Keep a record of this agency with their contact info and update it as necessary.

Name

[ ]   [ ]
First   Last

Address

[ ]
Street Address

[ ]   [ ]
City   State / Province / Region

[ ]
Postal / Zip Code

Email Address

[ ]

Phone Number

[ ] – [ ] – [ ]
####

Add items to your Transition Notebook

Add a flier or agency brochure to your Notebook.

. . . .

Guardianship Attorney

Keep a record of this agency with their contact info and update it as necessary.

Name

First	Last

Address

Street Address

City	State / Province / Region

Postal / Zip Code

Email Address

Phone Number

[   ] – [   ] – [   ]

####

Add a flier or agency brochure to your Notebook.

· ·

Job Coach

Keep a record of this agency with their contact info and update it as necessary.

Name

First	Last

Address

Street Address

City	State / Province / Region

Postal / Zip Code

Email Address

[   ]

Phone Number

[   ] – [   ] – [   ]

   ###   ###   ####

Add a flier or agency brochure to your Notebook.

Counselor

Keep a record of this agency with their contact info and update it as necessary

Name

[   ]   [   ]

First   Last

Address

[   ]

Street Address

[   ]   [   ]

City   State / Province / Region

[   ]

Postal / Zip Code

Email Address

[   ]

Phone Number

[   ] – [   ] – [   ]

   ###   ###   ####

Add a flier or agency brochure to your Notebook.

Medicare Professional/Medical Coupons

Keep a record of this agency with their contact info and update it as necessary

Name

First	Last

Address

Street Address

City	State / Province / Region

Postal / Zip Code

Email Address

Phone Number

– ### –

Add items to your Transition Notebook

Add a flier or agency brochure to your Notebook.

. . . .

Agency Notes: (Write down some of you thoughts from agency meetings here.)

MyAgency Experiences

This is a place where you can give your personal thoughts and preferences about the agencies you work with and how you feel everything is going. Use it like a journal!

Name

First	Last

Date

[   ] / [   ] / [   ]
MM   DD   YYYY

Make a list of the agencies and the people with whom you are currently working.

Are you working with:
- *Vocational Rehabilitation?*
- *Job Coach?*
- *Job Developer?*
- *Housing Specialist?*
- *Recreation Specialist?*
- *Therapist?*

How do you feel it is going with these agency personnel?

Do you feel like you:
- *Have a good plan to work on?*
- *Understand the information and service provided?*
- *Are understood when you communicate preferences?*
- *Are able to contact them in a timely manner?*

Tell about some great experiences you have had with the agencies you are working with:

- *Were you able to accomplish the things you talked about?*
- *Were you able to be understood and feel like your voice was heard?*
- *Did they follow through with what you were hoping for?*

Tell about some negative experiences you have had with the agencies you are working with:

- *Did anything go wrong?*
- *Did you feel misunderstood?*
- *How do you think they could have done something differently?*

What really works well for you when working with agencies?

- *Do you have preferences for communication?*
- *Do you have timelines that you are hoping for?*
- *Do you need for agency providers to know specific information before you meet with them?*
- *Do you have preferences for the type of person you like to work with? (male/female, etc.)*

Key #13: "Manage Your Own Money"

MyMoney

MySSI Documentation (6-Month Record Sheet)
(See Appendix for perforated copy)

Use this to help you track your SSI information,
as well as your expenses using SSI funds.

. . . .

Name

First	Last

Date

[ ] / [ ] / [ ]
MM   DD   YYYY

. . . .

Date Ranges

What date ranges are you reporting here?

FROM:

[ ] / [ ] / [ ]
MM   DD   YYYY

TO:

[ ] / [ ] / [ ]
MM   DD   YYYY

. . . .

SSI Income Documentation

This is the section where you will attach a copy of your SSI income (for the past 6 months).

. . . .

Month #1

Keep expense records for all of month #1 here.

Date

[ ] / [ ] / [ ]
MM   DD   YYYY

Income/Check Amount: (How much did you receive in this month's check?)

$ [   ] . [   ]
Dollars · Cents

Expenses – Food & Housing: (How much did you spend total on this month's food and housing?)

$ [   ] . [   ]
Dollars · Cents

Expenses – All other (Clothing/Medical-Dental, Recreation, Personal Items, Miscellaneous): (What is the total amount you spent from your check on all other expenses?)

$ [   ] . [   ]
Dollars · Cents

SSI Income saved (or left over): Month #1

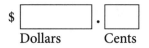
$ [   ] . [   ]
Dollars · Cents

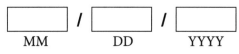

Add a copy of your SSI check to your Notebook.

Add Expense Sheet #1 to your Notebook. (Save an Excel worksheet or other file format to show the expenses you incurred during this particular month, and the payments made.)

• •

Month #2

Keep expense records for all of month #2 here.

Date

[   ] / [   ] / [   ]
MM DD YYYY

Income/Check Amount: (How much did you receive in this month's check?)

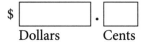
$ [   ] . [   ]
Dollars · Cents

Expenses – Food & Housing: (How much did you spend total on this month's food and housing?)

$ [   ] . [   ]
Dollars · Cents

Expenses – All other (Clothing/Medical-Dental, Recreation, Personal Items, Miscellaneous): (What is the total amount you spent from your check on all other expenses?)

$ [   ] . [   ]
Dollars   Cents

SSI Income saved (or left over): Month #2

$ [   ] . [   ]
Dollars   Cents

Add a copy of your SSI check to your Notebook.

Add Expense Sheet #2 to your Notebook. (Save an Excel worksheet or other file format to show the expenses you incurred during this particular month, and the payments made.)

Month #3

Keep expense records for all of month #3 here.

Date

[   ] / [   ] / [   ]
MM   DD   YYYY

Income/Check Amount: (How much did you receive in this month's check?)

$ [   ] . [   ]
Dollars   Cents

Expenses – Food & Housing: (How much did you spend total on this month's food and housing?)

$ [   ] . [   ]
Dollars   Cents

Expenses – All other (Clothing/Medical-Dental, Recreation, Personal Items, Miscellaneous): (What is the total amount you spent from your check on all other expenses?)

$ [   ] . [   ]
Dollars   Cents

SSI Income saved (or left over): Month #3

$ [   ] . [   ]
Dollars   Cents

Add a copy of your SSI check to your Notebook.

Add Expense Sheet #3 to your Notebook. (Save an Excel worksheet or other file format to show the expenses you incurred during this particular month, and the payments made.)

Month #4

Keep expense records for all of month #4 here.

Date

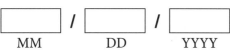

MM / DD / YYYY

Income/Check Amount: (How much did you receive in this month's check?)

$ [ ] . [ ]
Dollars Cents

Expenses – Food & Housing: (How much did you spend total on this month's food and housing?)

$ [ ] . [ ]
Dollars Cents

Expenses – All other (Clothing/Medical-Dental, Recreation, Personal Items, Miscellaneous): (What is the total amount you spent from your check on all other expenses?)

$ [ ] . [ ]
Dollars Cents

SSI Income saved (or left over): Month #4

$ [ ] . [ ]
Dollars Cents

Add a copy of your SSI check to your Notebook.

Add Expense Sheet #4 to your Notebook. (Save an Excel worksheet or other file format to show the expenses you incurred during this particular month, and the payments made.)

Month #5

Keep expense records for all of month #5 here.

Date

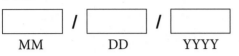

MM / DD / YYYY

Income/Check Amount: (How much did you receive in this month's check?)

$ [____] . [__]
Dollars   Cents

Expenses – Food & Housing: (How much did you spend total on this month's food and housing?)

$ [____] . [__]
Dollars   Cents

Expenses – All other (Clothing/Medical-Dental, Recreation, Personal Items, Miscellaneous): (What is the total amount you spent from your check on all other expenses?)

$ [____] . [__]
Dollars   Cents

SSI Income saved (or left over): Month #5

$ [____] . [__]
Dollars   Cents

Add a copy of your SSI check to your Notebook.

Add Expense Sheet #5 to your Notebook. (Save an Excel worksheet or other file format to show the expenses you incurred during this particular month, and the payments made.)

Month #6

Keep expense records for all of month #6 here.

Date

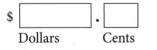

MM / DD / YYYY

Income/Check Amount: (How much did you receive in this month's check?)

$ [____] . [__]
Dollars   Cents

Expenses – Food & Housing: (How much did you spend total on this month's food and housing?)

$ [ ] . [ ]
Dollars   Cents

Expenses – All other (Clothing/Medical-Dental, Recreation, Personal Items, Miscellaneous): (What is the total amount you spent from your check on all other expenses?)

$ [ ] . [ ]
Dollars   Cents

SSI Income saved (or left over): Month #6

$ [ ] . [ ]
Dollars   Cents

Add a copy of your SSI check to your Notebook.

Add Expense Sheet #6 to your Notebook. (Save an Excel worksheet or other file format to show the expenses you incurred during this particular month, and the payments made.)

• •

6–Month Totals

Find the totals of expense categories for the last 6-month period.

Total Amount of SSI Benefits Received for this 6-Month Period: (Add all of the SSI checks for this period, and enter the total amount here.)

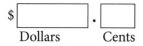
$ [ ] . [ ]
Dollars   Cents

Total Amount for Food and Housing for this 6-Month Period: (Put this amount on line 3B of form SSA 623.)

$ [ ] . [ ]
Dollars   Cents

Total Expenses for Clothing/Medical-Dental, Recreation, Personal Items, Miscellaneous: (Put this amount on line 3C of form SSA 623.)

$ [ ] . [ ]
Dollars   Cents

Show the total amount you SAVED for the beneficiary, including interest earned: (Subtract all expenses from the total benefit received, and add this figure to line 3D on form SSA 623.)

$ [ ] . [ ]
Dollars   Cents

MyBudget (See Appendix for perforated copy)

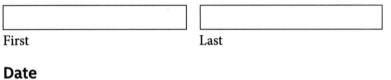

This is a plan for your budgeting needs.
Use it to guide you toward well-managed money.

• •

Name

First _____   Last _____

Date

[ ] / [ ] / [ ]
MM   DD   YYYY

• •

General Budget Considerations

Let's make some general choices for your planned budget.

How often do you review your budget?

Do you review and update your budget:
- *once a week?*
- *once a month?*
- *when a job is completed?*

How often do you get paid?

❑ Once a week
❑ Every 2 weeks
❑ Once per month
❑ When a job is completed
❑ Other

Check off all your major expense categories to plan your budget.

❑ Housing
❑ Utilities
❑ Food
❑ Entertainment
❑ Transportation
❑ Clothing
❑ Medical/Health
❑ Personal: Education/Gifts/Hair/Misc.
❑ Debts
❑ Other

Let's now write down some specific numbers!

This is a section for your expected expenses, and a review of what you've spent in general categories.

How much will you spend on HOUSING? (You should have tracked your expenses, or you could estimate what you spent. Enter amount for this category and all the following categories):

$ [＿＿＿] . [＿＿]
Dollars   Cents

How much did you spend on this last month?

$ [＿＿＿] . [＿＿]
Dollars   Cents

How much will you spend on UTILITIES?

$ [＿＿＿] . [＿＿]
Dollars   Cents

How much did you spend on this last month?

$ [＿＿＿] . [＿＿]
Dollars   Cents

How much will you spend on FOOD?

$ [＿＿＿] . [＿＿]
Dollars   Cents

How much did you spend on this last month?

$ [＿＿＿] . [＿＿]
Dollars   Cents

How much will you spend on ENTERTAINMENT?

$ [＿＿＿] . [＿＿]
Dollars   Cents

How much did you spend on this last month?

$ [＿＿＿] . [＿＿]
Dollars   Cents

How much will you spend on TRANSPORTATION?

$ [＿＿＿] . [＿＿]
Dollars   Cents

How much did you spend on this last month?

$ [＿＿＿] . [＿＿]
Dollars   Cents

How much will you spend on CLOTHING?

$ [＿＿＿] . [＿＿]
Dollars   Cents

How much did you spend on this last month?

$ [＿＿＿] . [＿＿]
Dollars   Cents

How much will you spend on MEDICAL/HEALTH?

$ [＿＿＿＿] . [＿＿]
Dollars   Cents

How much did you spend on this last month?

$ [＿＿＿＿] . [＿＿]
Dollars   Cents

How much will you spend on PERSONAL/MISC.?

$ [＿＿＿＿] . [＿＿]
Dollars   Cents

How much did you spend on this last month?

$ [＿＿＿＿] . [＿＿]
Dollars   Cents

How much will you spend on DEBT REPAYMENT?

$ [＿＿＿＿] . [＿＿]
Dollars   Cents

How much did you spend on this last month?

$ [＿＿＿＿] . [＿＿]
Dollars   Cents

How much will you spend on OTHER?

$ [＿＿＿＿] . [＿＿]
Dollars   Cents

How much did you spend on this last month?

$ [＿＿＿＿] . [＿＿]
Dollars   Cents

. . . .

Your Completed Budget

Go ahead and show what your current budget looks like here.

Add items to your Transition Notebook

Add a copy of your current budget to your Notebook. (You can find great forms online for your budgeting needs. Simply fill one out, save as a .pdf and print it out.)

MyWallet

This is a place where you can keep track of what you need in your wallet.

Hmmm...What's in MY wallet?

• •

Name

First	Last

Date

MM	DD	YYYY

• •

What kind of wallet do you like to have?
❑ Small for my pocket
❑ Medium for coins, bills, cards
❑ Large for checks, coins, bills and cards

What are some things that you like to have in your wallet?

❑ Driver's License   ❑ Debit Card   ❑ Credit Cards
❑ Emergency Cash   ❑ Personal I.D.   ❑ Rewards Cards
❑ Current Coupons   ❑ Checks   ❑ Coins
❑ Emergency Contact Info ❑ Health Insurance Card ❑ Auto Insurance Card

How much cash should you keep on you for emergencies?

$ [   ] . [   ]
   Dollars   Cents

Keep these in a safe place, not in your wallet!
❑ Social Security Card
❑ Birth Certificate
❑ PIN Numbers
❑ Passwords
❑ Spare Keys
❑ Blank Checks
❑ Extra Credit Cards
❑ Gift Cards - Unless you will use it
❑ Passport
❑ Medicare Card

What is your plan to stay organized with your wallet contents?

- *How will you keep extra receipts?*
- *How will you keep a log of expenses?*
- *When will you make copies of your wallet contents?*
- *Who can you talk to about staying organized with money?*

What is the money management app that you could use on your cell phone?

- *mvelopes.com*
- *goodbudget.com*
- *myweeklybudget.com*

What is your plan if you lose your wallet?

Who should you call?
- *A caregiver?*
- *Your bank to report your card?*
- *The last place you might have left it?*
- *The main office at school or work?*

Key #14: "Enjoy Your Independence"

My Independence

MyGrocery List (*See Appendix for perforated copy*)

Use this section to keep track of your standard grocery list.

Add a standard shopping list that works for you to your Notebook. (You can find standard grocery lists on the internet. Just download them or create .pdf and print. Or, you can use these selections below as a simple guideline.)

Select some things you may need to have on your list:

❑ Apples
❑ Bananas
❑ Grapefruit
❑ Grapes
❑ Lemons
❑ Melon
❑ Oranges
❑ Pears
❑ Pineapple
❑ Strawberries
❑ Broccoli
❑ Carrots
❑ Celery
❑ Corn
❑ Cucumbers
❑ Green Peppers
❑ Lettuce
❑ Mushrooms
❑ Onions
❑ Potatoes
❑ Tomatoes
❑ Zucchini
❑ Beef
❑ Chicken
❑ Fish
❑ Hamburger
❑ Hot Dogs

❑ Lunch Meat
❑ Apple Sauce
❑ Bagels
❑ Baked Beans
❑ Burritos
❑ Canned Fruit
❑ Canned Nuts
❑ Cereal
❑ Cheese
❑ Frozen Waffles
❑ Fruit Snacks
❑ Garlic Bread
❑ Granola Bars
❑ Hamburger Helper
❑ Macaroni and Cheese
❑ Noodles
❑ Pizza
❑ Potato Chips
❑ Rice
❑ Tuna
❑ Yogurt
❑ Tortilla Chips
❑ Croutons
❑ Jelly
❑ Ketchup
❑ Mayonnaise
❑ Mustard

❑ Peanut Butter
❑ Pickles
❑ Pasta Sauce
❑ Pizza Sauce
❑ Salad Dressing
❑ Salsa
❑ Taco Shells
❑ Butter
❑ Flour
❑ Oil
❑ Pancake Mix
❑ Sugar
❑ Syrup
❑ Coffee
❑ Creamer
❑ Fruit Juice
❑ Milk
❑ Tea
❑ Cling Wrap
❑ Foil
❑ Lunch Bags
❑ Napkins
❑ Paper Towels
❑ Toilet Paper
❑ Light Bulbs

MyLiving Space

This section helps you describe preferences for your living space.

Name

First	Last

Date

	/		/	
MM		DD		YYYY

Your Living Space Layout

Describe where you like to have furniture and other things in your personal living space.

How important is the layout for your room or other living spaces?

❑ Very Important

❑ Important

❑ Somewhat Important

❑ Not at all Important

❑ N/A

What would you like people to know about your room or personal living space?

- *Do you like your furniture a certain way?*
- *Do you have things in your room that help you to feel comfortable?*

How do you feel about other people being in your room or personal living space?

- *Are there things that people shouldn't touch?*
- *Are there things in your personal space that are very sentimental?*
- *If someone wants to be in your living space, are there times that are okay with you? Times that are not?*

(Continued from previous page.)

Do you need:
- *Special lighting?*
- *A quiet space?*
- *Fabrics that work best for you?*

What are some things to consider for your home?

- *Do you need a lock for your door?*
- *Do you need someone to help make sure you are safe?*
- *Do you need help to establish boundaries to protect your space?*

Add a picture of your room as you like it to your Notebook! (Take a picture of your room cleaned up, or with things where you like them to be.)

Security Measures: What do you need in order to be safe in your living space?

Are there some things you would change about your space?

- *What would you like to buy?*
- *What would you like to do to make it more safe?*
- *What would you change about the layout?*
- *Would you want to paint?*

How would you rate your current room/living space?

★ ★ ★ ★ ★ **(Circle or highlight your star rating)**

MyRoommates

This is a place where you can share your preferences for roommates and sharing your living space with others.

Name

First	Last

Date

MM / DD / YYYY

Address

Street Address

City	State / Province / Region

Postal / Zip Code

Email Address

Phone Number

– ### –

Add items to your Transition Notebook

Add a picture of yourself with your roommate(s) to your Notebook. (Attach a fun picture of you with your roommates or people who share your living space.)

Add a copy of your current budget to your Notebook. (You can find generic contracts online or at an office supply store.)

How much do you pay per month for rent? (Write in your portion of the rent.)

$ [　　　　] . [　　]
Dollars　　Cents

How do you feel about having roommates (rate how you feel)

★★★★★ (Circle or highlight your star rating)

What type of living situation are you currently in?

[　　　　　　　　　　　　　　　　　]

Do you live in...
- *Your family home?*
- *An apartment?*
- *An adult group home?*
- *A dorm room?*
- *Other?*

Describe your current living situation here!

[　　　　　　　　　　　　　　　　　]

- *What is your home like?*
- *Is it large or small?*
- *Do you like it?*
- *Are there things you would change?*

How often to you interact or hangout with your roommate(s)?
- ❏ Everyday
- ❏ Once a week
- ❏ 2 to 3 times a month
- ❏ Once a month
- ❏ Less than once a month

How often do you WANT to hang out with your roommate(s)
- ❏ Everyday
- ❏ Once a week
- ❏ 2 to 3 times a month
- ❏ Once a month
- ❏ Less than once a month

Who are your roommates?

[ ]

- *How did you meet them?*
- *Where did you meet?*
- *How is your relationship with them?*
- *Are there things that you love about them?*
- *Are there some issues you would like to work out?*

What are the utilities you split with roommates:

❏ Gas/Electricity

❏ Water/Sewer

❏ Cable/Internet

❏ Other

What are your financial obligations/agreements you have with your roommates?

[ ]

Detail out your agreements here.
- *What did you agree to?*
- *What are the amounts?*
- *When do you pay bills?*

What is the website for your apartment community (if applicable)?

(Find the website for the current apartment community where you live. Write the URL here.)

[ ]

Do you or any of your roommates have renters insurance?

[ ]

*Renters insurance is **very important** in protecting you from loss or damage of the things you own. It isn't very expensive, and can help you in case of theft or damage.*

A Mediator: If I have a problem, I can call...

This is a place to note who you could call if you need help working out your living situation.

Who can you call if you have a problem with a roommate and need help?

This could be...
- *A family member*
- *A close friend*
- *A counselor*

Mediator's Phone Number

####

Mediator's Phone Number

####

Additional Information:

What would you like to add about your roommate situation? Use this space to answer freely.
- *What are the things that you really want/need from a roommate?*
- *What are some ways that you can best get along with other roommates?*
- *What kind of communication needs do you have?*

MyVacation Plans

This form will help you to plan some of the things you will want for your vacation.Everyone should have the opportunity to do the things they love. Let's do this!

· ·

Name

First	Last

Date

[MM] / [DD] / [YYYY]

· ·

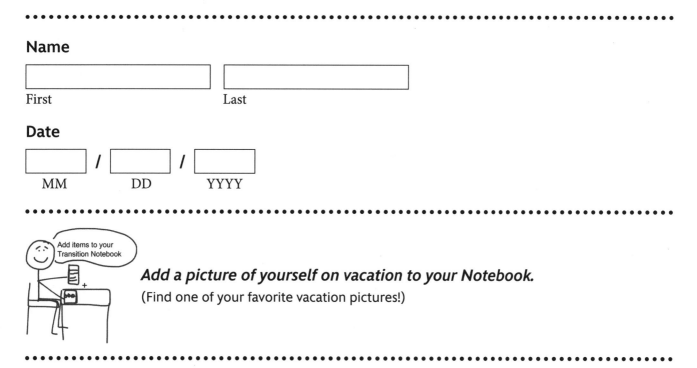

Add a picture of yourself on vacation to your Notebook.
(Find one of your favorite vacation pictures!)

· ·

About your vacation preferences:

Fill in some information to tell about what you would like to do for your next vacation.

Where do you want to go for this vacation?

What place are we talking about...
- *An amusement park?*
- *A different city?*
- *A different state?*
- *A different country?*

Website of your vacation spot (Is there a website URL for the place you would like to visit?):

What are the dates of your vacation? (Type in a date range, and use the format: mm/dd/yyyy - mm/dd/yyyy)

Why do you want to spend your vacation this way?

You may have a "stay-cation" or you might be planning on going somewhere. What are you ready to do differently so that you can get some rest?

Who will you be with for this vacation?

This may be with:
- *Family*
- *Friends*
- *Coworkers*
- *By yourself*

What are you most looking forward to? (Pick one, two or several of these choices.)

❑ Just relaxing

❑ Travel to see new things

❑ Have an adventure and some fun

❑ Spend time outdoors

❑ Be with the people I love

❑ Try something new

❑ Be sporty

❑ Gather some new information (e.g., college visits)

MyVacation Budget

How much will you need to spend for:
- *Airfare?*
- *Hotel or other place to stay?*
- *Rental car (or shared cost)?*
- *Food for each day?*

ADD IT UP! Write down your estimated costs.

What will I need to pack for my trip? (If you are planning a "day-trip," simply type N/A.)

Write down all of the things you can think of that you might need to buy and/or pack for your trip.

Add a "MyPacking List" document to your Notebook. (You can attach a document from a list you have found useful from the internet. Or, you can use the checklist in the "MyLuggage" section of this potfolio.)

Dream Big! Use this space to write some EPIC travel plans:

This is an opportunity to really dream big!!!!

What is your biggest dream when it comes to travel and vacation plans?
  - *What will it take for you to reach this dream?*

MyTravel Budget

This is a place where you are able to plan for the expenses of your trip.

Name

First	Last

Date

[ ] / [ ] / [ ]
MM   DD   YYYY

Airfare Total: (Write the total cost of airfare including taxes and fees.)

$ [ ] . [ ]
Dollars   Cents

Hotel: (Per Night) x (Number of Nights) = (Go ahead and do the math on a calculator and then enter the total cost here.)

$ [ ] . [ ]
Dollars   Cents

Taxi/Rental Car Total: (Make sure you estimate what this cost might be, including a tip for the driver if you are taking a cab.)

$ [ ] . [ ]
Dollars   Cents

Entertainment Total: (Think about the things you would like to do for fun on your trip. Do you want to go on some tours or special events?)

$ [ ] . [ ]
Dollars   Cents

Fuel Total: (If you are renting a car, estimate the price of gas for the trip. (Total Miles) x (Price/Gal) =?)

$ [ ] . [ ]
Dollars   Cents

Food Total: (Eating out? Buying food at the store? Bringing some food with you? (Number of days) x (amount per day for all meals)

$ [ ] . [ ]
Dollars   Cents

• •

Your Total Travel Budget:

This is the estimated amount to save before your trip.

Estimated Total for This Trip: (Add all of the amounts above for your estimated budget and put the total amount here.)

$ [ ] . [ ]
Dollars   Cents

MyItinerary

Share some of your ideas for where you will go on your next trip and the timeline that you are expecting.

. . . .

Name

First	Last

Date

MM		DD		YYYY

. . . .

When will you be taking your trip?

What are the dates of your trip?

Date (What day will you be starting your trip?)

MM		DD		YYYY

Date (What day will you come home from your trip?)

MM		DD		YYYY

. . . .

Where will you be staying on your trip?

Write the name of the hotel, house, campground or other here.

Place #1 Address

Street Address

City	State / Province / Region

Postal / Zip Code	Country

Place #1 Phone Number

###　　　###　　　####

Place #1 Website – Write the URL (website address) of the place where you will be staying.

How much will it cost to stay per night?

$ [   ] . [   ]

Dollars　Cents

Place #2 Address

Street Address

City

State / Province / Region

Postal / Zip Code

Country

Place #2 Phone Number

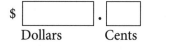

###　　　###　　　####

Place #2 Website – Write the URL (website address) of the place where you will be staying.

How much will it cost to stay per night?

$ [   ] . [   ]

Dollars　Cents

Transportation

This is where you can describe your plans for getting around.

To: What is your flight information? (What is the name of the airline and flight number going to your destination?)

From: What is your flight information? (What is the name of the airline and flight number for returning home from your trip?)

How do you intend to get around? (What type of transportation will you be taking? Check all that apply.)

❑ Airplane   ❑ Train   ❑ Taxi
❑ Personal Car   ❑ Public Bus   ❑ Shuttle

Other Transportation? (Is there a way that you will travel that was not available above?)

• •

MyMaps and Schedules

This is a place where you can keep any maps or schedules that you are needing for your trip.

Add items to your Transition Notebook

Add a map of the area where you will be traveling to your Notebook. (Print a .jpg or .pdf file to attach, showing the place you will be traveling. Attach a schedule that you will need to have on your trip. You may need to save this while planning.)

Timetable/Bus Schedule #1 - Add as next page in your Notebook.

Timetable/Bus Schedule #2 - Add as next page in your Notebook.

Draw or attach a map of the place you are going:

MyLuggage

If you are planning to go on a trip, you can use this section to keep track of your luggage needs.

● ●

Name

First	Last

Date

[   ] / [   ] / [   ]
MM   DD   YYYY

● ●

Add items to your Transition Notebook

Add a picture of yourself with your luggage to your Notebook. (Find a great picture of you going on a trip!)

Pack This!!! (Select some things that you will need to have on your trip.)

❑ Earplugs	❑ Sleeping Mask	❑ Travel Pillow
❑ Personal I.D.	❑ Wallet/Money	❑ Travel Docs
❑ Underwear	❑ Socks	❑ Sleepwear
❑ Tank Tops	❑ Jeans	❑ Shorts
❑ Dress Pants	❑ Dress Shirts	❑ Ties
❑ Jewelry	❑ Skirts	❑ Dress/Suit
❑ Shoes	❑ Flip Flops	❑ Slippers
❑ Exercise Clothes	❑ Raincoats	❑ Hats
❑ Belts	❑ Swimsuit	❑ Towel
❑ Robe	❑ Sunglasses	

Pack This - Hygiene!!! (Select some things that you will need for your own personal hygiene on your trip.)

❑ Shampoo	❑ Conditioner	❑ Hair Gel
❑ Hairspray	❑ Comb/Brush	❑ Make-up Remover
❑ Razor	❑ Shaving Cream	❑ Mouthwash
❑ Toothpaste	❑ Toothbrush	❑ Cologne/Perfume
❑ Make-up	❑ Lotion	❑ Bandaids
❑ Sunscreen	❑ Bug Repellant	❑ Deodorant

Pack This - Entertainment!!! (Select some things that you will need to stay entertained during down-time on your trip.)

❑ Computer	❑ iPod	❑ Tablet
❑ Books	❑ Magazines	❑ Video Games
❑ Camera	❑ Toys	❑ Travel Journal
❑ Sketch Book	❑ Pens/Pencils	❑ Maps
❑ Binoculars	❑ Flashlight	❑ Travel Book

Pack This - Comfort!!! (Select some things that you will need to stay comfortable on your trip.)

❑ Sleeping Bag	❑ Pillow	❑ Air Mattress
❑ Comforter	❑ Stress Reliever	❑ Anti-Nausea Medicine
❑ Medications	❑ Gloves	❑ Hand Warmers
❑ Hand-Held Fan	❑ Water Bottle	❑ Chapstick/Lipgloss

What type of trip are you planning for?

❑ Road Trip
❑ Airplane Trip
❑ Train Trip
❑ Cruise
❑ Trip to Amusement Park
❑ Tropical Island/Beach
❑ Adventure/Active
❑ Nature Exploration
❑ Museum Tour
❑ College Tour
❑ Sports Related Vacation

Additional items to pack:

MyNotes

Use these pages for notes or drawings.

MyNotes

MyNotes

MyNotes

MyNotes

MyNotes

Appendix

My Transition Portfolio Companion Notebook

Use this list to help you organize your own Companion Notebook

••

MyPersonal Information (A Person-Centered Profile)
- ❑ MyPermission to Treat
- ❑ MyNutrition Plan
- ❑ MyEmergency Care Plan
- ❑ MyExercises
- ❑ MyWorkout Program
- ❑ MyWork/School Schedule
- ❑ MyPersonal Schedule

Key #1 MyDream
- ❑ MyDream Pictures

Key #2 MyStory
- ❑ MyBirthplace Map
- ❑ MyBaby Pictures
- ❑ MyToy Pictures
- ❑ MyElementary School Picture
- ❑ MyJunior High School Picture
- ❑ MyHigh School Pictures
- ❑ MyPicture Journal
- ❑ MyFamily Pictures
- ❑ MyPet Pictures
- ❑ MyFamily Tree
- ❑ MyFriends Pictures

Key #3 MyCommunication
- ❑ MyCommunication Device
- ❑ MyCommunication Device Usage
- ❑ MyPotential Communication Device

Key #4 MySelfie and MyFavorities
- ❑ MySelfie
- ❑ MyEvents
- ❑ MyFavorite Place
- ❑ MyTravel Goal
- ❑ MyBus Trips
- ❑ MyFavorite Games
- ❑ MyNew Games
- ❑ MySports
- ❑ MyPersonal Style
- ❑ MyCelebrities
- ❑ MyHair Cuts

Key #5 MySelf Assessments
- ❑ MyStrengths Charts

Key #6 MyCareer Research
- ❑ MyResume
- ❑ MyInterview Cards

Key #7 MyTransition Plans
- ❑ MyCurrent Transition Plan

Key #8 MyIEP and Transcripts
- ❑ MyIEP
- ❑ MyStudent-Led IEP
- ❑ MyTranscripts

Key #9 MyCulminating Project
- ❑ MyScript
- ❑ MyMovie Project

Key #10 MyGraduation and Adult Life
- ❑ MyGraduation Pictures
- ❑ MyGraduation Announcements

Key #11 MyWork Information
- ❑ MyVocational Assessments
- ❑ MyVocational Evaluations

Key #12 MyAdult Service Agencies
- ❏ MyCase Manager
- ❏ MyHousing Specialist
- ❏ MyVocational Rehab
- ❏ MyEmployment Agency
- ❏ MyGuardianship
- ❏ MyJob Coach
- ❏ MyCounselor
- ❏ MyDoctors

Key #13 MyMoney
- ❏ MySSI Expense Sheets
- ❏ MyBudget

Key #14 MyIndependence
- ❏ MyShopping List
- ❏ MyRoom
- ❏ MyRoommates
- ❏ MyVacation Pictures
- ❏ MyPacking List
- ❏ MyTravel Maps/Schedules
- ❏ MyLuggage

Miscellaneous Documents
- ❏ MyIncentive Charts
- ❏ MySocial Solutions
- ❏ MyPocket Resume
- ❏ MyPocket Profile

Vocational Portfolio Quiz

Name

First	Last

Date

[ ] / [ ] / [ ]
MM   DD   YYYY

1. What is your full name? _____

2. What is your phone number? _____

3. What is your address? _____

4. What is a pocket resume? How can you use it in the future? _____
_____

5. What does your "MyDream Statement" tell about you? _____
_____

6. From "MyStory"—What was life like for you when you were you were a little kid? ____
_____

7. Where do you want to live some day? _____

8. When will you graduate from high school? _____

9. What will you do for fun when you are an adult? _____

10.What makes you REALLY happy right now? _____

11.What is a "reference" on your resume? _____

12.What does "gender" mean? What is your gender? _____

13. What are three of you greatest strengths? _____
_____
_____
_____

14. Why would you be good at the job you are choosing for your dream statement? _____

_____

15.What makes you a good friend to people? _____

_____

_____

_____

_____

16. Why do you think you will make a great employee in the future?

MyVocational Evaluation (Example)

. . . .

Worksite: _____

Job: _____

Name: _____

Month: _____

Job Coach: _____

General

1. Puts personal belongings away in proper place	Yes ❑	No ❑	Emerging Skill ❑	N/A ❑
2. Greets co-workers/friendly	Yes ❑	No ❑	Emerging Skill ❑	N/A ❑
3. Checks in, gets assignment	Yes ❑	No ❑	Emerging Skill ❑	N/A ❑
4. Friendly to members	Yes ❑	No ❑	Emerging Skill ❑	N/A ❑
5. Completes weekly time sheets	Yes ❑	No ❑	Emerging Skill ❑	N/A ❑

Cleaning

6. Uses & changes cleaning cloths, as instructed	Yes ❑	No ❑	Emerging Skill ❑	N/A ❑
7. Uses proper cleaner for glass, pink cleaner for other surfaces	Yes ❑	No ❑	Emerging Skill ❑	N/A ❑
8. Applies spray to surfaces or cloths, as instructed	Yes ❑	No ❑	Emerging Skill ❑	N/A ❑
9. Wipes tables systematically	Yes ❑	No ❑	Emerging Skill ❑	N/A ❑
10. Straightens chairs	Yes ❑	No ❑	Emerging Skill ❑	N/A ❑
11. Tidies objects in the work environment	Yes ❑	No ❑	Emerging Skill ❑	N/A ❑
12. Wipes window sills	Yes ❑	No ❑	Emerging Skill ❑	N/A ❑
13. Sanitizes door handles throughout facility	Yes ❑	No ❑	Emerging Skill ❑	N/A ❑
14. Sanitizes all railings	Yes ❑	No ❑	Emerging Skill ❑	N/A ❑
15. Sanitizes drinking fountain handles and buttons	Yes ❑	No ❑	Emerging Skill ❑	N/A ❑

Cleans windows & other glass, inside & out, streak free

16. Lobby	Yes ❑	No ❑	Emerging Skill ❑	N/A ❑
17. Front door	Yes ❑	No ❑	Emerging Skill ❑	N/A ❑
18. Other entrance door	Yes ❑	No ❑	Emerging Skill ❑	N/A ❑
19. Sanitizes door handles throughout facility	Yes ❑	No ❑	Emerging Skill ❑	N/A ❑
20. Sanitizes stairway railing	Yes ❑	No ❑	Emerging Skill ❑	N/A ❑

Wipes down equipment

21. Works from bottom to top	Yes ❑	No ❑	Emerging Skill ❑	N/A ❑
22. Works systematically	Yes ❑	No ❑	Emerging Skill ❑	N/A ❑
23. Cleans equipment thoroughly	Yes ❑	No ❑	Emerging Skill ❑	N/A ❑
24. Selects equipment to be cleaned next, as instructed	Yes ❑	No ❑	Emerging Skill ❑	N/A ❑

Conduct

25. General conduct acceptable to this workplace	Yes ❑	No ❑	Emerging Skill ❑	N/A ❑
26. Absent rate below 9%	Yes ❑	No ❑	Emerging Skill ❑	N/A ❑
27. Grooming & hygiene	Yes ❑	No ❑	Emerging Skill ❑	N/A ❑
28. Clothing appropriate to this worksite	Yes ❑	No ❑	Emerging Skill ❑	N/A ❑

Communication & Problem Solving

29. Shows good work ethic, energy & enthusiasm	Yes ❑	No ❑	Emerging Skill ❑	N/A ❑
30. Customer service (or task completion) knowledge, manners	Yes ❑	No ❑	Emerging Skill ❑	N/A ❑
31. Polite & friendly to staff (knows names)	Yes ❑	No ❑	Emerging Skill ❑	N/A ❑
32. Requests accommodations as needed	Yes ❑	No ❑	Emerging Skill ❑	N/A ❑
33. Remembers instructions & details	Yes ❑	No ❑	Emerging Skill ❑	N/A ❑
34. Follows chain of command for questions, general info, etc.	Yes ❑	No ❑	Emerging Skill ❑	N/A ❑
35. Knows location of equipment & supplies	Yes ❑	No ❑	Emerging Skill ❑	N/A ❑
36. Knows layout of worksite	Yes ❑	No ❑	Emerging Skill ❑	N/A ❑
37. Adjusts own work-speed for specific task & workload	Yes ❑	No ❑	Emerging Skill ❑	N/A ❑
38. Sets up an efficient workspace	Yes ❑	No ❑	Emerging Skill ❑	N/A ❑
39. Evaluates & adjusts for quality of own work	Yes ❑	No ❑	Emerging Skill ❑	N/A ❑

Safety

40. Uses proper equipment & supplies for the task	Yes ❑	No ❑	Emerging Skill ❑	N/A ❑
41. Returns equipment & supplies to proper place	Yes ❑	No ❑	Emerging Skill ❑	N/A ❑
42. Handles spills safely & as instructed	Yes ❑	No ❑	Emerging Skill ❑	N/A ❑
43. Uses sharp tools safely & as instructed	Yes ❑	No ❑	Emerging Skill ❑	N/A ❑
44. Uses cleaners or chemicals safely & as instructed	Yes ❑	No ❑	Emerging Skill ❑	N/A ❑
45. Lifts safely & as instructed	Yes ❑	No ❑	Emerging Skill ❑	N/A ❑
46. Recognizes potential hazards	Yes ❑	No ❑	Emerging Skill ❑	N/A ❑

MyStory – A Letter to Caregivers

Student Name: _____

Date: _____

Dear Parents/Guardians:

In the next few weeks, our class will begin a unit called "MyStory." In this unit, we will be working with students to assist them in telling the story about their life's journey so far. We will be highlighting events from their early childhood and infants/toddlers, school years and young-adult experiences. The information gathered in this process will then be shared through essay writing and in opportunities to give voice to their own life experiences.

We have provided students a questionnaire which contains prompts to guide their thoughts as they reflect on specific information that they want to share. It is our hope that you will be able to assist your student at home in recalling those experiences and that we will be able to build on individual stories in the classroom setting. We see this opportunity as a shared experience between the staff, students, and caregivers, but want to ensure that our students are able to independently communicate their own perspectives and deliver the information in whatever way works best for them and their communication style.

Please see the attached questionnaire and follow the prompts with your student as their homework assignment. We are excited to hear about any of the details from their personal history and will make sure that we keep any information confidential if so indicated by you. Thank you in advance for your participation in creating a rich and valuable perspective on the life of your student. This information will be kept in their developing portfolio and the final copy of their written essay will be sent home.

Please indicate below any information that you would like to share or anything that you would prefer to keep confidential.

All the best!

Information from Parent/Guardian:

MyStory Questionnaire
Assisted by Parent/Caregiver

Use this fillable form to gather information about your life: Past, Present, and Future. You will have an opportunity to use this information in your "All About Me" narrative.

•••

Name

[   ] [   ]
First   Last

Date

[   ] / [   ] / [   ]
MM   DD   YYYY

•••

Early Childhood Years...

Where were you born?

- *What was the hospital name?*
- *What city/state?*
- *What were the other conditions on the day your were born?*

[   ]

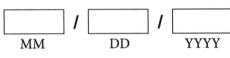

Add a map of the place you were born to your Notebook. (You can use a web-based map to show where you were born or raised. Attach your printed map or picture of where you were born.)

When were you born? (Do you know the exact time you were born?)

[   ] : [   ] [   ]
HH   MM   AM/PM

What were you like as a baby?

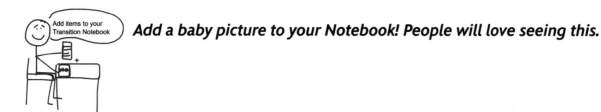

- *What do you see from pictures or hear about yourself from parents/caregivers?*
- *What was your personality like?*

Add a baby picture to your Notebook! People will love seeing this.

What were your favorite things as a baby?

Favorite toys?

Add a picture of your favorite toy to your Notebook.
(You were no doubt adorable!!!)

....

Elementary School Years...

Describe what you remember about pre-school and elementary school here.

Did you go to a pre-school? If so, where?

What elementary school did you go to? (Do you remember the name of the school?)

What do you remember about elementary school?

| |
| |

- *Best friends?*
- *Favorite games/toys?*
- *Teachers?*

Add an elementary school picture to share and remember where you went to school to your Notebook.

• •

Junior High Years...

What was the name of your junior high or middle school?

| |

What was your favorite thing about junior high school? ...and least favorite?

| |
| |

Junior high school can be very difficult, but it can also be very fun.

What are your memories from that time?

Did you have a favorite teacher?

| |
| |

- *Who was the teacher? Why were they your favorite?*
- *What did they help you to do or learn?*
- *Have you ever stayed in contact with them?*
- *Is there anything else you can add?*

Favorite subject in junior high:

- *Math*
- *English*
- *PE*
- *Art*
- *Social Studies*

MyTransition from junior high to high school:

Describe your experiences moving from junior high to high school.

Were you...Nervous? Scared? Excited? Happy?

Add items to your Transition Notebook

Add a junior high picture to your Notebook, too!

High School Years

What high school did you go to?

What was your sophomore year like?

- *Classes*
- *Teachers*
- *Friends*
- *Sports*

What was your junior year like? Or, what do you hope it will be like?

[ ]

- *Classes*
- *Teachers*
- *Friends*
- *Sports*
- *Clubs*

What was your senior year like? Or, what do you hope it will be like?

[ ]

- *Classes*
- *Teachers*
- *Friends*
- *Sports*
- *Graduation planning*

Add a picture from high school to your Notebook...this could be a dance, sports or the school itself.

• •

MyFuture Goals

Write about two goals you have for the future here.

[ ]

What would you like to have happen in your life?

Are there some things that you would like to change?

(Brainstorm Here)

Goal #1 (Write your goal titles or domain areas here.)

Goal #2

Use this example if you would like!

Example:
By _____, I would like to be able to _____.
In the future, I would also really like to _____

MyJournal Entries

MyJournal

Use this space to write some of your thoughts down:

• •

Name

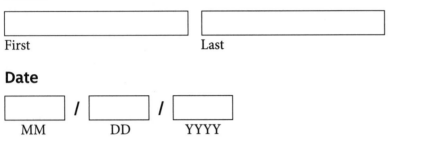

First   Last

Date

[   ] / [   ] / [   ]

MM   DD   YYYY

• •

Describe a current problem here:

What could be a potential solution to this problem or situation?

Journal Entry/Notes   Date: ___/___/_____

Teachers/Caregivers:

Please make copies of this page as needed for additional entries.

Journal Entry/Notes   Date: ___/___/_____

Journal Entry/Notes   Date: ___/___/_____

MyWeekend Plans

Name

First	Last

Date

MM	DD	YYYY

My favorite part of the week was:

My plan for this weekend is:

Friday Night:

For dinner I would like to have: _____

I will stay up until: _____

Watch a movie: Yes ❏ / No ❏ If so, which one? _____

A friend I could call _____ Their phone # _____

I would like to go to: _____

If I go there, I will: _____

Saturday:

For breakfast I would like to have: _____

For lunch I would like to have: _____

For dinner I would like to have: _____

I will stay up until: _____

Watch a movie: Yes ❏ / No ❏ If so, which one? _____

A friend I could call _____ Their phone # _____

I would like to go to: _____

If I go there, I will: _____

Sunday:

For breakfast I would like to have: _____

For lunch I would like to have: _____

For dinner I would like to have: _____

I will stay up until: _____

Watch a movie: Yes ❏ / No ❏ If so, which one? _____

A friend I could call _____ Their phone # _____

I would like to go to: _____

If I go there, I will: _____

My plan for transportation this weekend:

How are you planning on getting to the things you want to do this weekend?

- *Ask a parent/caregiver?*
- *Carpool with someone?*
- *Share rides to and from?*
- *Take the bus?*
  - —*What bus or buses?*
  - —*What times?*

How much money will you need for the events you are planning?

- *Will you need to pay to get in?*
- *Will you be ordering something to eat?*
- *Will you need money for the bus?*

Add everything up!

MyTrip Planner

Name

First	Last

Date

	/		/	
MM		DD		YYYY

1. **Where would you like to go in the community?** (Examples are parks, specialty stores, exhibits, exercise facilities, recreational opportunities, etc.)

2. **Why are you interested in going there?**

3. **Who would you want to go with for this trip?**

4. **What are the hours of the places/businesses you would like to go to? Will they be open during the times you want to visit?** (Confirm this by calling or looking up hours online.)

5. **What bus (or buses) do I need to take to get there?**

6. **What time does the bus leave?**

7. **What is my plan for lunch? Am I going to bring lunch from home or buy one in the community?**

8. **What supplies do I need to bring on this outing? How much money do I need?**

MyStudent-Led IEP Meeting

This activity will help you to pan for your IEP meeting.
You can use this to help guide you in leading a portion of your
own meeting... It's all about YOU!

Name

First	Last

Date

MM	/	DD	/	YYYY

Introduction

Who is at your meeting?

- **You:**
- **Case Manager:**
- **District Representative:**
- **Parent/Guardian:**
- **DVR Counselor:**
- **Employment Vendor:**

Purpose of the Meeting

We are meeting today to go over my progress on goals, my transition plan, and my future goals.

My current goals are:

The accommodation that I get in my classes for texts are:

Vision for the Future

What do you want for your life in these areas:

- Career:
- Family:
- Housing:
- Transportation:
- Fun/Friends/
Recreation:

· ·

Goals

How have you done on your goals with your current IEP?

What are the goals that you would like to be working on this next year?

· ·

Learning Style

My learning style is important for others to know. When an idea or work is presented to me, I have found that it is best if people know more about my style.

My best learning style is...

❑ Visual Learner: Watching

❑ Kinesthetic: Feeling/Doing

❑ Auditory: Listening

❑ Multi-Sensory: Several modes

I learn new skills best when people:

❑ Show me what to do.

❑ Let me work with my hands, feel it and try it.

❑ Just tell me how to do something and let me try.

❑ Use different ways: Show me, let me try it, and tell me as well.

My Portfolio

Here is my current portfolio

In it, you will see:

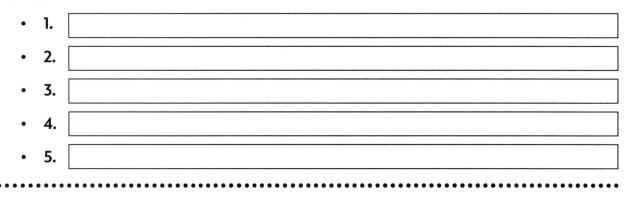

- 1.
- 2.
- 3.
- 4.
- 5.

My Case Manager:

My IEP is written, updated and reported on by:

[   ]

- I would now like for my case manager to talk about some of the details of my plan.

- We will show the team a copy of my IEP.

- Thank you for being here!

Additional information/notes from MyIEP Meeting:

MyParagraph Development

Use the graphic below to organize your writing for your Career Research Report Outline.

Name

First		Last

Date

	/		/	
MM		DD		YYYY

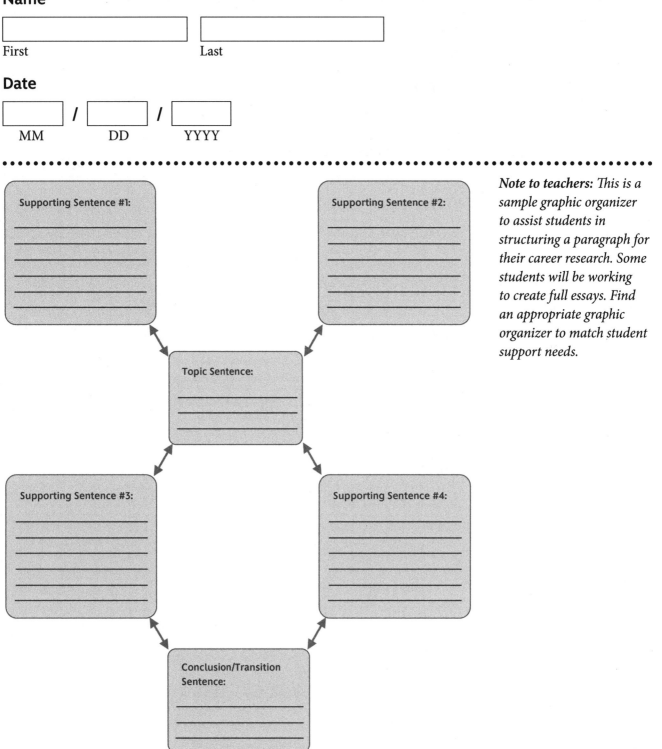

Supporting Sentence #1:
_____
_____
_____
_____
_____

Supporting Sentence #2:
_____
_____
_____
_____
_____

Topic Sentence:
_____
_____
_____

Supporting Sentence #3:
_____
_____
_____
_____
_____

Supporting Sentence #4:
_____
_____
_____
_____
_____

Conclusion/Transition Sentence:
_____
_____
_____

Note to teachers: This is a sample graphic organizer to assist students in structuring a paragraph for their career research. Some students will be working to create full essays. Find an appropriate graphic organizer to match student support needs.

MySSI Documentation (6-Month Record Sheet)

Use this to help you track your SSI information,
as well as your expenses using SSI funds.

· ·

Name

First　　　　　　　　　　　　Last

Date

[　　] / [　　] / [　　]
　MM　　　DD　　　YYYY

· ·

Date Ranges

What date ranges are you reporting here?

FROM:

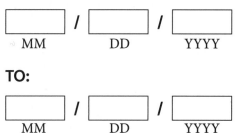

[　　] / [　　] / [　　]
　MM　　　DD　　　YYYY

TO:

[　　] / [　　] / [　　]
　MM　　　DD　　　YYYY

· ·

SSI Income Documentation

This is the section where you will attach a copy of your SSI income (for the past 6 months).

· ·

Month #1

Keep expense records for all of month #1 here.

Date

[　　] / [　　] / [　　]
　MM　　　DD　　　YYYY

Income/Check Amount: (How much did you receive in this month's check?)

$ [   ] . [   ]
Dollars   Cents

Expenses – Food & Housing: (How much did you spend total on this month's food and housing?)

$ [   ] . [   ]
Dollars   Cents

Expenses – All other (Clothing/Medical-Dental, Recreation, Personal Items, Miscellaneous): (What is the total amount you spent from your check on all other expenses?)

$ [   ] . [   ]
Dollars   Cents

SSI Income saved (or left over): Month #1

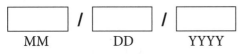
$ [   ] . [   ]
Dollars   Cents

Add a copy of your SSI check to your Notebook.

Add Expense Sheet #1 to your Notebook. (Save an Excel worksheet or other file format to show the expenses you incurred during this particular month, and the payments made.)

Month #2

Keep expense records for all of month #2 here.

Date

[   ] / [   ] / [   ]
MM   DD   YYYY

Income/Check Amount: (How much did you receive in this month's check?)

$ [   ] . [   ]
Dollars   Cents

Expenses – Food & Housing: (How much did you spend total on this month's food and housing?)

$ [   ] . [   ]
Dollars   Cents

Expenses – All other (Clothing/Medical-Dental, Recreation, Personal Items, Miscellaneous): (What is the total amount you spent from your check on all other expenses?)

$ [   ] . [   ]
Dollars   Cents

SSI Income saved (or left over): Month #2

$ [   ] . [   ]
Dollars   Cents

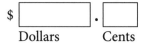
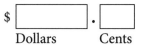

Add items to your Transition Notebook

Add a copy of your SSI check to your Notebook.

Add Expense Sheet #2 to your Notebook. (Save an Excel worksheet or other file format to show the expenses you incurred during this particular month, and the payments made.)

Month #3

Keep expense records for all of month #3 here.

Date

[   ] / [   ] / [   ]
MM   DD   YYYY

Income/Check Amount: (How much did you receive in this month's check?)

$ [   ] . [   ]
Dollars   Cents

Expenses – Food & Housing: (How much did you spend total on this month's food and housing?)

$ [   ] . [   ]
Dollars   Cents

Expenses – All other (Clothing/Medical-Dental, Recreation, Personal Items, Miscellaneous): (What is the total amount you spent from your check on all other expenses?)

$ [   ] . [   ]
Dollars   Cents

SSI Income saved (or left over): Month #3

$ [   ] . [   ]
Dollars   Cents

Add a copy of your SSI check to your Notebook.

Add Expense Sheet #3 to your Notebook. (Save an Excel worksheet or other file format to show the expenses you incurred during this particular month, and the payments made.)

•••

Month #4

Keep expense records for all of month #4 here.

Date

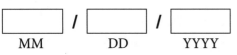

MM   DD   YYYY

Income/Check Amount: (How much did you receive in this month's check?)

$ ☐ . ☐
Dollars   Cents

Expenses – Food & Housing: (How much did you spend total on this month's food and housing?)

$ ☐ . ☐
Dollars   Cents

Expenses – All other (Clothing/Medical-Dental, Recreation, Personal Items, Miscellaneous): (What is the total amount you spent from your check on all other expenses?)

$ ☐ . ☐
Dollars   Cents

SSI Income saved (or left over): Month #4

$ ☐ . ☐
Dollars   Cents

Add a copy of your SSI check to your Notebook.

Add Expense Sheet #4 to your Notebook. (Save an Excel worksheet or other file format to show the expenses you incurred during this particular month, and the payments made.)

•••

Month #5

Keep expense records for all of month #5 here.

Date

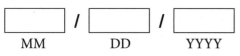

MM   DD   YYYY

Income/Check Amount: (How much did you receive in this month's check?)

Dollars   Cents

Expenses – Food & Housing: (How much did you spend total on this month's food and housing?)

Dollars   Cents

Expenses – All other (Clothing/Medical-Dental, Recreation, Personal Items, Miscellaneous): (What is the total amount you spent from your check on all other expenses?)

Dollars   Cents

SSI Income saved (or left over): Month #5

Dollars   Cents

 *Add a copy of your SSI check to your Notebook.*

Add Expense Sheet #5 to your Notebook. (Save an Excel worksheet or other file format to show the expenses you incurred during this particular month, and the payments made.)

• •

Month #6

Keep expense records for all of month #6 here.

Date

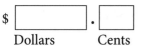

MM   DD   YYYY

Income/Check Amount: (How much did you receive in this month's check?)

$ ☐ . ☐

Dollars   Cents

Expenses – Food & Housing: (How much did you spend total on this month's food and housing?)

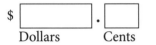
$ _____ . ___
Dollars   Cents

Expenses – All other (Clothing/Medical-Dental, Recreation, Personal Items, Miscellaneous): (What is the total amount you spent from your check on all other expenses?)

$ _____ . ___
Dollars   Cents

SSI Income saved (or left over): Month #6

$ _____ . ___
Dollars   Cents

Add items to your Transition Notebook

Add a copy of your SSI check to your Notebook.

Add Expense Sheet #6 to your Notebook. (Save an Excel worksheet or other file format to show the expenses you incurred during this particular month, and the payments made.)

• •

6–Month Totals

Find the totals of expense categories for the last 6-month period.

Total Amount of SSI Benefits Received for this 6-Month Period: (Add all of the SSI checks for this period, and enter the total amount here.)

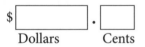
$ _____ . ___
Dollars   Cents

Total Amount for Food and Housing for this 6-Month Period: (Put this amount on line 3B of form SSA 623.)

$ _____ . ___
Dollars   Cents

Total Expenses for Clothing/Medical-Dental, Recreation, Personal Items, Miscellaneous: (Put this amount on line 3C of form SSA 623.)

$ _____ . ___
Dollars   Cents

Show the total amount you SAVED for the beneficiary, including interest earned: (Subtract all expenses from the total benefit received, and add this figure to line 3D on form SSA 623.)

$ _____ . ___
Dollars   Cents

MyBudget

This is a plan for your budgeting needs.
Use it to guide you toward well-managed money.

∙∙

Name

First	Last

Date

[MM] / [DD] / [YYYY]

∙∙

General Budget Considerations

Let's make some general choices for your planned budget.

How often do you review your budget?

Do you review and update your budget:
- *once a week?*
- *once a month?*
- *when a job is completed?*

How often do you get paid?

❏ Once a week
❏ Every 2 weeks
❏ Once per month
❏ When a job is completed
❏ Other

Check off all your major expense categories to plan your budget.

❏ Housing
❏ Utilities
❏ Food
❏ Entertainment
❏ Transportation
❏ Clothing
❏ Medical/Health
❏ Personal: Education/Gifts/Hair/Misc.
❏ Debts
❏ Other

Let's now write down some specific numbers!

This is a section for your expected expenses, and a review of what you've spent in general categories.

How much will you spend on HOUSING? (You should have tracked your expenses, or you could estimate what you spent. Enter amount for this category and all the following categories):

$ [_____] . [____]
Dollars   Cents

How much did you spend on this last month?

$ [_____] . [____]
Dollars   Cents

How much will you spend on UTILITIES?

$ [_____] . [____]
Dollars   Cents

How much did you spend on this last month?

$ [_____] . [____]
Dollars   Cents

How much will you spend on FOOD?

$ [_____] . [____]
Dollars   Cents

How much did you spend on this last month?

$ [_____] . [____]
Dollars   Cents

How much will you spend on ENTERTAINMENT?

$ [_____] . [____]
Dollars   Cents

How much did you spend on this last month?

$ [_____] . [____]
Dollars   Cents

How much will you spend on TRANSPORTATION?

$ [_____] . [____]
Dollars   Cents

How much did you spend on this last month?

$ [_____] . [____]
Dollars   Cents

How much will you spend on CLOTHING?

$ [_____] . [____]
Dollars   Cents

How much did you spend on this last month?

$ [_____] . [____]
Dollars   Cents

How much will you spend on MEDICAL/HEALTH?

$ [   ] . [   ]
Dollars   Cents

How much did you spend on this last month?

$ [   ] . [   ]
Dollars   Cents

How much will you spend on PERSONAL/MISC.?

$ [   ] . [   ]
Dollars   Cents

How much did you spend on this last month?

$ [   ] . [   ]
Dollars   Cents

How much will you spend on DEBT REPAYMENT?

$ [   ] . [   ]
Dollars   Cents

How much did you spend on this last month?

$ [   ] . [   ]
Dollars   Cents

How much will you spend on OTHER?

$ [   ] . [   ]
Dollars   Cents

How much did you spend on this last month?

$ [   ] . [   ]
Dollars   Cents

· ·

Your Completed Budget

Go ahead and show what your current budget looks like here.

Add items to your Transition Notebook

Add a copy of your current budget to your Notebook. (You can find great forms online for your budgeting needs. Simply fill one out, save as a .pdf and print it out.)

MyGrocery List

Use this section to keep track of your standard grocery list.

●●

Add a standard shopping list that works for you to your Notebook. (You can find standard grocery lists on the internet. Just download them or create .pdf and print. Or, you can use these selections below as a simple guideline.)

Select some things you may need to have on your list:

❑ Apples	❑ Lunch Meat	❑ Peanut Butter
❑ Bananas	❑ Apple Sauce	❑ Pickles
❑ Grapefruit	❑ Bagels	❑ Pasta Sauce
❑ Grapes	❑ Baked Beans	❑ Pizza Sauce
❑ Lemons	❑ Burritos	❑ Salad Dressing
❑ Melon	❑ Canned Fruit	❑ Salsa
❑ Oranges	❑ Canned Nuts	❑ Taco Shells
❑ Pears	❑ Cereal	❑ Butter
❑ Pineapple	❑ Cheese	❑ Flour
❑ Strawberries	❑ Frozen Waffles	❑ Oil
❑ Broccoli	❑ Fruit Snacks	❑ Pancake Mix
❑ Carrots	❑ Garlic Bread	❑ Sugar
❑ Celery	❑ Granola Bars	❑ Syrup
❑ Corn	❑ Hamburger Helper	❑ Coffee
❑ Cucumbers	❑ Macaroni and Cheese	❑ Creamer
❑ Green Peppers	❑ Noodles	❑ Fruit Juice
❑ Lettuce	❑ Pizza	❑ Milk
❑ Mushrooms	❑ Potato Chips	❑ Tea
❑ Onions	❑ Rice	❑ Cling Wrap
❑ Potatoes	❑ Tuna	❑ Foil
❑ Tomatoes	❑ Yogurt	❑ Lunch Bags
❑ Zucchini	❑ Tortilla Chips	❑ Napkins
❑ Beef	❑ Croutons	❑ Paper Towels
❑ Chicken	❑ Jelly	❑ Toilet Paper
❑ Fish	❑ Ketchup	❑ Light Bulbs
❑ Hamburger	❑ Mayonnaise	
❑ Hot Dogs	❑ Mustard	

MyIncentives Plan - Data Collection System

Student Name: _____

Case Manager: _____ Date(s): _____

Target Behavior: _____

Instructions: Offer points to student for targeted positive behavior(s). The student will then cash in points daily for short-term rewards, or on Friday for an allowed preferred activity. **No more than 5 points per data cell.**

	Monday	Tuesday	Wednesday	Thursday	Friday
Time Period 1					
Time Period 2					
Time Period 3					
Time Period 4					
Time Period 5					
Time Period 6					

Daily Totals: _____ _____ _____ _____ _____

Weekly Point Total: _____

Weekly Reward Schedule:

15 points – Earns: _____

30 points – Earns: _____

45 points – Earns: _____

MySocial Solutions

Name: _____

Date: _____

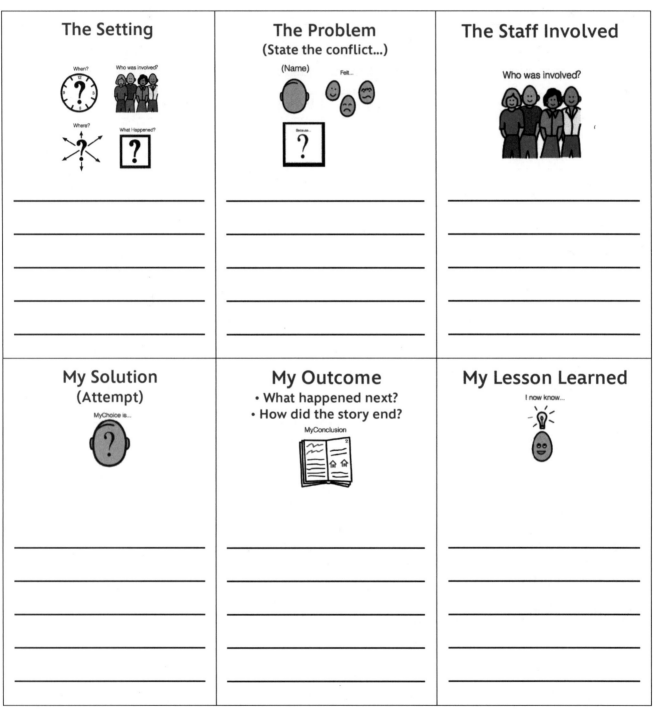

The Setting

When?   Who was involved?

Where?   What Happened?

_____

_____

_____

_____

_____

The Problem
(State the conflict...)

(Name)   Felt...

Because...

_____

_____

_____

_____

_____

The Staff Involved

Who was involved?

_____

_____

_____

_____

_____

My Solution
(Attempt)

MyChoice is...

_____

_____

_____

_____

My Outcome
• What happened next?
• How did the story end?

MyConclusion

_____

_____

_____

_____

My Lesson Learned

I now know...

_____

_____

_____

_____

Key Transition Planning

Consider this timeline when establishing plans for transition to adulthood.

Adulthood

Ages 18-21

- Register with Department of Vocational Rehabilitation
- Connect with an Employment Vendor (job coaching or job development)

Age 18

- Apply for SSI
- ReEval with Disability Services
- Activate Guardianship
- Enroll in Adult Transition Program (if available)
- Register for Selective Service

Ages 14-16

- Establish/Confirm Eligibility for State and County
- Start IEP Transition Planning
- Establish Financial Trust
- Prepare for Guardianship
- Community Bus Experiences/Practice Money Handling
- Volunteering

Ages 5-13

- Chore Charts
- Visual Schedules
- Positive Behavior Support
- Community-Based Activites and Camps

Note to Caregiver/Parent: *These are general suggestions of activities to accomplish at various stages of transition. Please only use them as a guideline. MyKey™ Consulting Services, LLC recognizes that every individual experiences their own unique set of circumstances which require thoughtful guidance by care teams.*

My Personal Feedback to the Author

Congratulations!

I'm so proud of you for taking the time to use these special keys to unlock the doors leading to your own self-determined future! It's been such a privilege for me to be able to help you discover and open up to others your greatest potential!

Now, I would love to know what you think of this portfolio which was created with you in mind. You, too, can make this journey better for others by giving me your feedback. These are my last questions for you:

• •

1) RATING: On a scale of 1 to 10, how would you rate the effectiveness of *"My Transition Portfolio"*? Please tell me why you chose this number.

2) Are you able to tell others about the Dream Statement you created?

3) As you move toward fulfilling your Dream Statement, do you fool like you have the supports you need? (Do you have the lifestyle planning and support to get there? What do you need to help you move toward the dream you have for yourself and your own life?)

4) Can you think of any forms that I should add?

• •

I'm looking forward to hearing from you soon! You can either provide your name or remain anonymous, your choice! Please email me your comments: barb@mykeyplans.com. Remember, "the best is yet to come!"